# The Family Business

# The Family Business

**Sarah Gale**, LLB
Solicitor, Lecturer in Law, City University

**Gary Scanlan**, LLB
Solicitor, Senior Lecturer in Law, City University

**Butterworths**
London, Edinburgh and Dublin
1998

| | |
|---|---|
| United Kingdom | Butterworths, a Division of Reed Elsevier (UK) Ltd, Halsbury House, 35 Chancery Lane, LONDON WC2A 1EL and 4 Hill Street, EDINBURGH EH2 3JZ |
| Australia | Butterworths, SYDNEY, ADELAIDE, BRISBANE, CANBERRA, MELBOURNE and PERTH |
| Canada | Butterworths Canada Ltd, TORONTO and VANCOUVER |
| Ireland | Butterworth (Ireland) Ltd, DUBLIN |
| Malaysia | Malayan Law Journal Sdn Bhd, KUALA LUMPUR |
| New Zealand | Butterworths of New Zealand Ltd, WELLINGTON and AUCKLAND |
| Singapore | Reed Elsevier (Singapore) Pte Ltd, SINGAPORE |
| South Africa | Butterworths Publishers (Pty) Ltd, DURBAN |
| USA | Michie, CHARLOTTESVILLE, Virginia |

© Reed Elsevier (UK) Ltd 1998

All rights reserved. No part of this publication may be reproduced in any material form (including photocopying or storing it in any medium by electronic means and whether or not transiently or incidentally to some other use of this publication) without the written permission of the copyright owner except in accordance with the provisions of the Copyright, Designs and Patents Act 1988 or under the terms of a licence issued by the Copyright Licensing Agency Ltd, 90 Tottenham Court Road, London, England W1P 0LP. Applications for the copyright owner's written permission to reproduce any part of this publication should be addressed to the publisher.

Warning: The doing of an unauthorised act in relation to a copyright work may result in both a civil claim for damages and criminal prosecution.

Any Crown copyright material is reproduced with the permission of the Controller of Her Majesty's Stationery Office.

A CIP Catalogue record for this book is available from the British Library.

ISBN 0 406 90138 4

Typeset by M Rules, London
Printed and bound in Great Britain by Redwood Books, Trowbridge, Wilts

**Visit us at our website: http://www.butterworths.co.uk**

# Preface

The importance of the family business as a source of employment and wealth cannot be underestimated; nevertheless it remains undefined by English law. The members of such an enterprise may, however, conduct their business either as a partnership or through the medium of a private limited company registered under the Companies Acts.

This book examines the advantages and disadvantages that flow from the selection of either of these forms of business organisation by the members of a family business. The traditional view is that the limited liability company is preferable to partnership. Those who take that view see for the private limited company fiscal advantages coupled with the ability of the members to limit their liability. These assumptions are ripe for re-examination.

We have sought therefore to compare the private limited company with the partnership as a means of carrying on a family business. Included in these comparisons are the position of the minority member in the family business, and the consequences that flow from the death of a member of a family business whether in an incorporated or un-incorporated form. We have by necessity been selective in our coverage of these issues.

The book has been written for the family member of either a partnership or a company, or those persons contemplating the formation of a family business. We hope that the busy general practitioner called upon to advise his client on such matters will find some value in this book.

The book is one of a new series which includes Austin Moore's books on the small business organisation in particular *Business Purchase* and *The Owner-Managed Business*. These books may address some of the issues that we could not raise in this book.

In conclusion, we come to the most pleasant part of writing a book, the opportunity to thank those who have helped in its production. First we must thank the editorial staff at Butterworths, who as always have been their usual model of professionalism and courtesy. Thanks must go to Michael Gale QC, Joanna Gale and Kim Scanlan who continue to provide support and encouragement and the occasional observation on our work.

We have sought to state the law as at 1 January 1998.

SG/GS

February 1998

# Contents

Preface v
Table of statutes xiii
Table of statutory instruments xvii
Table of cases xix

**Chapter 1 Formation of a business – partnership or company? 1**

Introduction 1
Limited liability 1
Financing the business 2
Fiscal advantages 2
Comparative costs of operating a family business 3
   Accounts 4
Exemptions and exceptions to the accounting requirements 4
   Small and medium-sized companies 4
Form of abbreviated accounts and reports 5
   Medium-sized companies 5
   Small companies 5
   Dispensing with laying accounts 6
Company auditors 6
   Conclusion 6
Incorporation 7
   Selling of business in whole or in part 7
Hiving off parts of a business 7
Mergers 8
Discrimination and social welfare legislation 9
Restraint of trade 9
   Conclusion 10

**Chapter 2 Operating the enterprise 12**

Running the business – the partnership 12
The right to participate in partnership affairs 12
Partnership decisions – partnership agreement 13
Special majorities 13

Determination of majority  14
Provision for partnership meetings  14
Accounts  14
Partners' duties  14
Prescribed duties  15
Indemnities  16
Death or retirement of a partner  16
Retirement  16
Bankruptcy  17
Expulsion  17
Consequences of termination  18
Dissolution and winding up  18
Pensions  18
Insurance  19
Illness or pregnancy of partners  19
Arbitration  19
Mediation  20
The family company  20
Directors  20
Articles of Association  21
Reversion of powers to the shareholders  21
Managing Director  22
Duties of the director  22
Fiduciary duties  22
The rules against profiting  23
Duties to individual shareholders  23
English authority  24
Duties between shareholders  25
Circumstances in which shareholders must vote in the best interests of the company  25
Directors – financial provision  26
Termination of office  26
Retirement  27
Removal  27
Pre-emption rights  28
Authority of directors  30
Conclusion – shareholder agreements  30
Contents of shareholder agreements  30
Conclusions  32

## Chapter 3  Divorce and the family business  33

The business as family property  33
The divorce settlement and the family business  33
Periodical payments  34
   Unsecured payments  35
   Secured payments  35
Tax implications  35
Lump sum payments  36
   Raising the funds  36
Director's remuneration  37

Dividends  38
Partnerships  38
Purchase by a company of its own shares  38
Fiscal consequences of acquisition  39
Partnerships  40
Sale of shares to a third party  40
Partnerships  41
Matrimonial disputes – family company directors/shareholders/spouses  42
Conclusion  43
Circumstances in which the court may not grant a lump sum order  43
Transfer and settlement of property orders  44
Variation of ante-nuptial and post-nuptial settlements  44
Orders for the sale of property  45
Consent orders  45
Conclusion  46
Liquidation of a company  46
Members' voluntary liquidation  46
   Nature of declaration  47
   Resolution for voluntary winding up  48
   Appointment of a liquidator  48
Creditors' voluntary a liquidation  49
   Liquidation committee  49
Compulsory liquidation  50
Circumstances in which a company may be wound up  51
The appointment of a provisional liquidator  51
Winding up of a company: commencement  52
Dissolution  52
   On completion of voluntary liquidation  52
The family partnership – winding up  53
   Dissolution under the Partnership Act 1890  53
   Dissolution by order of the court  53
Dissolution by notice  54
Winding up of partnership  55
   Post-dissolution profits  55
Distribution of partnership assets and adjustment of
    partnership accounts  55
The rule in *Garner v Murray*  56
Insolvent partnerships  56
Conclusion  57


**Chapter 4  Death and the family business**  58

Death and the family company  58
Death of a controlling shareholder  59
Death and the family partnership  60
The creditors of a partnership  61
Debts incurred by a partnership after a partner's death  62
Personal representatives admitted as partners  62
The separate creditors of the deceased partner's estate and beneficiaries  63
Loans to the partnership  64
Bequest of partnership share  66

x  *Contents*

Life interests  67
Life interests and the family company  68
Winding up of the family business on death of a member  68
Conclusions  69

**Chapter 5   Minority protection**  70

The partnership and the minority partner  70
Unanimous decisions: majority voting  70
   Admission of a new partner  70
Partners' duties  71
Management  71
Unanimity  72
Expulsion of a partner  73
Good faith  74
Injunctions  74
Appointment of a receiver/manager  75
Conclusion  76
Dissolution  76
Dissolution by court order  76
Conclusion  77
The minority shareholder in the family company  78
Special majorities  78
Director's duties  79
Action against directors  79
Fraud on the minority by those in control  80
   The concept of control  80
Fraud  80
Companies Act 1985, s 459  81
Orders under a petition  82
Meaning of interest  83
Unfairly prejudicial  84
*Re Harmer Ltd*  85
Just and equitable ground for winding up a company under the Insolvency
   Act 1986, s 122(1)(g)  85
Conclusion  86
The shareholder agreement  87

**Chapter 6   Winding up and insolvency of family businesses**  88

The insolvent partnership – insolvency procedures  88
Winding up of partnership as unregistered company  88
Winding up of insolvent partnership without concurrent petition  89
Parties who may present petition  89
Consequences of presentation of petition  89
Winding up order against insolvent partnership with
   concurrent petition(s)  89
Joint petition by all the partners to wind up the partnership  90
Petition for bankruptcy presented against one or more partners but with no
   attempt to wind up the partnership  90

The position of partners in the winding up of the partnership   91
The partner as contributor   91
Administration of partners and partnership estates   92
Expenses incurred by responsible insolvency practitioner   92
Priority of debts in joint estate   92
Priority of debts in separate estates   93
Priority of debts   93
  Conclusion   94
Voluntary arrangements   94
Administration orders   95
Conclusion   96
Corporate insolvency   96
Administrative receivership   96
Consequences of appointment of an administrative receiver   98
The receiver's powers   98
The receiver's duties   98
Administrative receiverships and company contracts   99
Priority of debts   99
Administration   100
The functions and purpose of the administrator   101
Creditors' meeting   101
Powers of the administrator   102
Priority of payment of debts   102
Voluntary arrangements   103
Approval of a proposal for a voluntary arrangement   104
Compulsory liquidation   105
Petitioners   105
Liquidation committee   106
Powers and duties of the liquidator   106
Priority of payment   107
Examination of transactions   107
Transactions at an undervalue – Insolvency Act 1986, s 238   108
Preferences – Insolvency Act 1986, s 239   108
Extortionate credit transactions – Insolvency Act 1986, s 244   109
Floating charges for past value – Insolvency Act 1986, s 245   109
Dispositions – Insolvency Act 1986, s 127   110
Transactions defrauding creditors – Insolvency Act 1986, s 423   110
  Fraudulent trading – Insolvency Act 1986, s 213   110
Wrongful trading – Insolvency Act 1986, s 214   111
Misfeance proceedings – Insolvency Act 1986, s 212   112
Conclusion   112

Index   115

# Table of statutes

References in this Table to *Statutes* are to Halsbury's Statutes of England showing the volume and page at which the annotated text of the Act will be found.

References in the right-hand column are to para numbers. References in **bold** type indicate where the section of an Act is set out in part or in full.

| | PARA |
|---|---|
| Administration of Estates Act 1925 (17 *Statutes* 302) | |
| s 33 (5), (7) | 4.32 |
| Charging Orders Act 1979 (22 *Statutes* 502) | 4.35 |
| Child Support Act 1991 (6 *Statutes* 294) | 3.11 |
| Companies Act 1948 | |
| s 28 | 2.59, 2.60 |
| 184 | 2.56 |
| Companies Act 1980 | 2.59 |
| Companies Act 1981 | 3.25 |
| Companies Act 1985 (8 *Statutes* 104) | 1.1, 5.26 |
| s 4, 28 | 2.36 |
| 80, 81, 89, 90 | 2.58 |
| 95 (1), (2) | 2.58 |
| 154 | 6.78 |
| 162 | 3.23 |
| 164(2), (5) | 2.48 |
| 171(1)-(3) | 3.23 |
| 183(3) | 4.2 |
| 187 | 4.2 |
| 213, 214 | 6.76 |
| 226 | 1.10 |
| 242(1) | 1.10 |
| 247(1) | 1.14 |
| (2) | 1.14, 1.15 |
| (3) | 1.14 |
| 303 | 2.53, 2.56, 5.51 |
| 312 | 2.50 |
| 313(1) | 2.50 |
| 316(3) | 2.50 |
| 317 | 2.42 |
| 320 | 2.36 |
| 359 | 2.61 |
| 360 | 4.34 |
| 366A | 1.18 |
| 378 | 3.53 |

| | PARA |
|---|---|
| Companies Act 1985—*contd* | |
| s 378 (1) | 5.28 |
| (2) | 3.49, 5.28 |
| 379A | 1.18 |
| 459 | 2.61, 3.36, 5.40, 5.43, 5.44, 5.45, 5.46, 5.49, 5.52 |
| (1) | 5.38, 5.41 |
| (2) | 4.2 |
| 460 | 2.61, 3.36 |
| 461 | 2.61, 3.36, 5.38, 5.43 |
| (2) | 5.41 |
| 711(1) | 3.68 |
| 716(1) | 1.28 |
| Sch 4 | |
| para 55 | 1.16 |
| Sch 6 | |
| para 7(1) | 2.50 |
| Sch 8 | |
| para 12 | 2.50 |
| 18, 20, 39 | 1.17 |
| Companies Act 1989 | |
| s 115 | 1.18 |
| Company Directors (Disqualification) Act 1986 (8 *Statutes* 781) | 6.11, 6.92 |
| s 10 | 6.88 |
| Finance Act 1982 (13 *Statutes* 444) | |
| Pt III (ss 13–19) | 3.26 |
| Finance Act 1988 (24 *Statutes* 633) | 3.11 |
| Finance Act 1989 (43 *Statutes* 989) | |
| s 104 | 3.16 |
| Income and Corporation Taxes Act 1988 (44 *Statutes* 1) | |
| s 20 | 1.7 |
| 337(2) | 1.7 |
| 414 | 3.16 |
| 660A | 3.12 |
| 660B | 3.13 |

xiv  *Table of statutes*

| | PARA |
|---|---|
| Inheritance (Provision for Family and Dependants) Act 1975 (17 *Statutes* 388) | 3.7 |
| Insolvency Act 1986 (4 *Statutes* 717) | 2.36, 6.32, 6.79 |
| Pt I (ss 1–7) | 6.26 |
| Pt V (ss 220–229) | 6.33 |
| Pt VIII (ss 252–263) | 6.5 |
| s 1 | 6.28, 6.60 |
| (3) | 6.63 |
| 2 (3) | 6.60 |
| 3 | 6.29 |
| 3 (2) | 6.63 |
| (10) | 6.60 |
| 4 (1), (3), (4) | 6.64 |
| (6) | 6.65 |
| 5 | 6.29 |
| (3), (4) | 6.67 |
| 6 | 6.65 |
| (4), (7) | 6.66 |
| 7 (4) (b) | 6.49, 6.69 |
| 8 (1) (a) | 6.50 |
| (2) | 6.49 |
| (4) | 6.50 |
| (13) | 6.49 |
| 9 (3) | 6.52 |
| 10 | 6.34 |
| (3) | 6.59 |
| 11 | 6.34 |
| (1) (a) | 6.68 |
| 12 | 6.35 |
| 13 | 6.36 |
| 14 | 6.55, 6.56 |
| 15 | 6.56 |
| 18 | 6.53 |
| 19 (6) | 6.56 |
| 22 | 6.56 |
| 24 (1), (5) | 6.54 |
| 26 (2) | 6.54 |
| 27 | 6.54 |
| 29 (1) | 6.39 |
| (2) | 6.39, 6.41 |
| 32 | 6.41 |
| 40 | 6.48 |
| (2) | 6.39 |
| 43 | 6.48, 6.56 |
| 44 | 6.82 |
| 47 | 6.43, 6.56 |
| 48 (2) | 6.45 |
| (3) (b) | 6.45 |
| (5) | 6.44 |
| 49 | 6.46 |
| 74 (2) (f) | 6.77 |
| 79 | 6.69 |
| 84 (1) (c) | 3.53 |
| 86 | 3.65 |
| 89 (1) | 3.50 |
| (2) (a) | 3.49 |
| (b) | 3.51 |
| (3) | 3.49 |
| (4), (5) | 3.51 |
| (6) | 3.49 |

| | PARA |
|---|---|
| Insolvency Act 1986—*contd* | |
| s 90 (2) | 3.55 |
| 91 (1) | 3.54 |
| 94 (3)–(5) | 3.68 |
| 100 | 3.58 |
| 101 | 3.59 |
| 103 | 3.60 |
| 106 (3)–(5) | 3.68 |
| 110 | 3.60 |
| 114 (3) | 3.56 |
| 122 (1) (a), (d) | 3.62 |
| (g) | 2.61, 3.62, 4.2, 5.51, 5.52 |
| 123 (1) (a) | 6.70 |
| (2) | 6.70 |
| 124 (1) | 6.69 |
| (2) | 6.8 |
| 127 | **6.86** |
| 129 (1) | 3.65 |
| (2) | 3.66, 6.6, 6.68 |
| 131 (1) | 6.14 |
| 139 (2), (3) | 6.72 |
| 140 (1), (2) | 6.71 |
| 141 (1) | 6.73 |
| 143 (1) | 6.74 |
| 146 | 3.69 |
| 148, 150, 154 | 6.13 |
| 160 (b), (d) | 6.13 |
| 165 (2) (b) | 3.60 |
| 166 | 3.58, 3.60 |
| 167 (1) (a) | 6.73 |
| 172 (8) | 3.69 |
| 175 | 6.18, 6.23, 6.75 |
| 175B (1) (b) | 6.21 |
| 175C | 6.18 |
| (2) | 6.23 |
| 201 (1) | 3.68 |
| 202 | 6.72 |
| (2), (3) | 3.68 |
| 205 (1)–(4) | 3.69 |
| 212 | 6.93 |
| 213 | 6.88, 6.89, 6.92 |
| 214 | 6.92 |
| (4), (5) | 6.91 |
| Pt V (ss 220–229) | 6.33 |
| s 221 (1) | 6.7 |
| (7) | 6.4, 6.11 |
| (8) | 6.7 |
| 221A (1) | 6.5 |
| 226 | 6.11 |
| (1), (2) | 6.12 |
| 228 | 6.13 |
| 234 | 6.14 |
| (1), (2) | 6.46 |
| 235 | 6.46 |
| 236 (4), (5) | 6.72 |
| 238 | 6.52, 6.81 |
| (5) | 6.80 |
| 239 | 6.52, 6.81 |
| 240 | 6.52, **6.80** |
| (3) | 6.81 |
| 241 | 6.80, 6.81 |

*Table of statutes* xv

| | PARA |
|---|---|
| Insolvency Act 1986—*contd* | |
| s 244 (3) | 6.82 |
| 245 | 6.52 |
| (3) | 6.84 |
| (4) | 6.85 |
| (6) | 6.83 |
| 247 (2) | 3.66 |
| 249 (4) | 6.82 |
| Pt VIII (ss 252–263) | 6.5 |
| s 264 | 6.9 |
| 272 (1) | 6.9 |
| 303 (2A)–(2C) | 6.10 |
| 328 | 6.18, 6.23 |
| 328A | 6.18 |
| 328B (1) (b) | 6.21 |
| s 328C (2) | 6.21 |
| 339 | 2.21 |
| 386 | 6.25 |
| 340 | 2.21 |
| 423 | 2.21, 6.87 |
| Sch 1 | 6.55 |
| Sch 4 | |
| para 1–3 | 3.60 |
| Sch 6 | 6.25, 6.75 |
| Sch 10 | 3.49, 3.51 |
| Insolvency Act 1994 | |
| s 1 (4) | 6.57 |
| 2 | 6.47 |
| Law of Property Act 1925 (37 *Statutes* 72) | |
| s 34 (2) | 1.21 |
| Limited Partnerships Act 1907 (32 *Statutes* 810) | 1.1, 3.16 |
| Matrimonial Causes Act 1973 (27 *Statutes* 734) | |
| s 21 | 3.5 |
| 23 | 3.42 |
| 24 | 3.43, 3.44 |
| 24A | 3.45 |
| 25 | 3.6, 3.46 |
| Matrimonial Homes and Property Act 1981 (27 *Statutes* 613) | |
| s 7 | 3.45 |

| | PARA |
|---|---|
| Partnership Act 1890 (32 *Statutes* 782): | 1.1, 2.1, 2.14, 3.75, 4.27, 5.18, 5.51, 6.95 |
| s 1 | 2.13 |
| 2 | 4.15 |
| (3) (d) | 6.25 |
| 3 | 6.18, 6.25 |
| 5 | 2.3, 2.35 |
| 8 | 2.3 |
| 10, 12 | 2.28 |
| 20 | 6.14 |
| 24 (1) | 3.80 |
| (5) | 2.2, 2.36, 2.37, 2.58 |
| (7) | 5.2 |
| (8) | **2.4**, 2.5, **5.5**, 5.6, 5.8 |
| 25 | 5.11 |
| 28 | 1.10 |
| 31 (1) | **3.32** |
| (2) | **3.35** |
| 33 | 5.23 |
| (1) | 2.18, 2.22, 4.9 |
| (2) | **3.71** |
| 34 | 5.23 |
| 35 (c) | 5.23 |
| (d) | 3.73, 5.23 |
| (e), (f) | 3.73 |
| 39 | 4.9 |
| 42 | 3.77, 4.11, 4.22, 4.24 |
| (2) | 4.25 |
| 44 | 3.78, 3.81, 3.82 |
| Pensions Act 1995 | 3.29 |
| Race Relations Act 1976 (6 *Statutes* 828) | |
| s 1 | 1.30 |
| 10 (1) | 1.30 |
| 73 | 1.30 |
| Sex Discrimination Act 1975 (6 *Statutes* 753) | 2.30 |
| Sex Discrimination Act 1986 | |
| s 1 (3) | 2.30 |

# Table of statutory instruments

References in the right-hand column are to para numbers.

| | PARA |
|---|---|
| Companies Act 1985 (Accounts of Small and Medium-Sized Enterprises and Publication of Accounts in ECUs) Regulations 1992, SI 1992/2452 | 2.50 |
| reg 5 | 1.14 |
| Companies Act 1985 (Audit Exemption) Regulations 1994, SI 1994/1935 | 1.19 |
| Companies (Tables A to F) Regulations 1985, SI 1985/805 | |
| Schedule | |
| Table A | |
| reg 5 | 4.34 |
| 31, 38 | 4.3 |
| 70 | 2.36, 5.30 |
| 72 | 2.38 |
| 73, 74 | 2.52 |
| 81 | 2.51 |
| 82 | 2.50 |
| 84 | 2.38, 2.52, 5.30 |
| 85 | 2.42, 5.30 |
| 86, 94 | 2.42 |
| County Court Rules 1981, SI 1981/1687 | |
| Order 12 | |
| r 1 (1) (b) | 4.18 |
| Insolvency Regulations 1986, SI 1986/1994 | |
| reg 27 (2) | 3.60 |
| Insolvency Rules 1986, SI 1986/1925 | |
| r 4.38 (4) | 3.60 |
| 4.62 (4) | 3.60 |

| | PARA |
|---|---|
| Insolvency Rules 1986—*contd* | |
| r 4.127, 4.155 | 3.60 |
| 4.168, 4.170, 4.183 | 3.60 |
| 4.195–198, 4.202 | 6.13 |
| 4.205 (2) | 6.13 |
| 4.221–222 | 6.13 |
| Insolvency (Amendment) Rules 1995, SI 1995/586 | 3.60 |
| Insolvent Partnerships Order 1994, SI 1994/2421 | 6.3, 6.5, 6.95 |
| art 4 | 6.26 |
| 7 | 6.4, 6.14 |
| 8 (1) | 6.7 |
| 10 | 6.8 |
| 11 | 6.9 |
| 14 (2) | 6.10 |
| Sch 1 | 6.26, 6.28 |
| Sch 2 | 6.32 |
| art 6 | 6.30 |
| Sch 3 | 6.4, 6.7, 6.14 |
| Sch 4 | 6.7, 6.11 |
| Sch 6 | 6.7, 6.8 |
| Sch 7 | 6.9 |
| Insolvent Partnerships (Amendment) Order 1996, SI 1996/1308 | |
| art 2 | 6.3 |
| Rules of the Supreme Court 1965, SI 1965/1776 | |
| Order 16 | |
| r 1 (1) (b) | 4.18 |
| Order 50 | |
| r 11–14 | 4.35 |

# Table of cases

PARA

**A**

A and BC Chewing Gum Ltd, Re, Topps Chewing Gum Inc v Coakley [1975] 1 All ER 1017, [1975] 1 WLR 579, 119 Sol Jo 233 .................................... 5.51
Aberdeen Rly Co v Blaikie Bros (1854) 2 Eq Rep 1281, [1843-60] All ER Rep 249, 23 LTOS 315, 1 Macq 461, HL................................................ 2.42
Alexander v Automatic Telephone Co [1900] 2 Ch 56, 69 LJ Ch 428, 48 WR 546, 44 Sol Jo 407, 82 LT 400, 16 TLR 339, CA ................................... 5.34
Allen v Gold Reefs of West Africa Ltd [1900] 1 Ch 656, 69 LJ Ch 266, 7 Mans 417, 48 WR 452, [1900-3] All ER Rep 746, 44 Sol Jo 261, 82 LT 210, 16 TLR 213, CA: 2.49
Allen v Hyatt (1914) 30 TLR 444, PC ........................................ 2.43
Alsager v Rowley (1802) 6 Ves 748 ........................................... 4.19
Atlantic Computer Systems plc, Re [1992] Ch 505, [1992] 1 All ER 476, [1992] 2 WLR 367, [1991] BCLC 606, [1990] BCC 859, CA ...................... 6.58

**B**

B v B (financial provision) [1989] FCR 146, [1989] 1 FLR 119, [1989] Fam Law 105, [1989] NLJR 186 ......................................................... 3.41
Backwell v Child (1755) Amb 260 ............................................. 4.31
Bagel v Miller [1903] 2 KB 212, 72 LJKB 495, 8 Com Cas 218, 88 LT 769, DC .... 4.14
Barnes v Youngs [1898] 1 Ch 414, 67 LJ Ch 263, 46 WR 332, 42 Sol Jo 269 ....... 5.13
Barron v Potter [1914] 1 Ch 895, 83 LJ Ch 646, 21 Mans 260, 58 Sol Jo 516, 110 LT 929, 30 TLR 401 ......................................................... 2.37
Beattie v E & F Beattie Ltd [1938] Ch 708, [1938] 3 All ER 214, 107 LJ Ch 333, 82 Sol Jo 521, 159 LT 220, 54 TLR 964, CA .................................... 5.45
Beningfield v Baxter (1886) 12 App Cas 167, 56 LJPC 13, 56 LT 127, PC ......... 4.19
Blisset v Daniel (1853) 10 Hare 493, 1 Eq Rep 484, 18 Jur 122, 1 WR 529 ......... 5.4
Blue Arrow plc, Re [1987] BCLC 585, 3 BCC 618 ............................. 5.45
Booth v Booth (1838) 1 Beav 125, 8 LJ Ch 39, 2 Jur 938, 49 RR 304 ............. 4.24
Bosworthick v Bosworthick [1927] P 64, 95 LJP 171, [1926] All ER Rep 198, 70 Sol Jo 857, 136 LT 211, 42 TLR 719, CA ....................................... 3.44
Bray v Fromont (1821) 6 Madd 5 ............................................. 1.25
Brazilian Rubber Plantations and Estates Ltd, Re [1911] 1 Ch 425, 80 LJ Ch 221, 18 Mans 177, 103 LT 697, 27 TLR 109 ...................................... 2.39
Briess v Woolley [1954] AC 333, [1954] 1 All ER 909, 98 Sol Jo 286, HL ......... 2.35
Browne v Collins (1871) LR 12 Eq 586 ....................................... 4.33
Bushell v Faith [1970] AC 1099, [1970] 1 All ER 53, [1970] 2 WLR 272, 114 Sol Jo 54, HL ...................................................................... 2.54
Byrne v Reid [1902] 2 Ch 735, 71 LJ Ch 830, 51 WR 52, 87 LT 507, CA ......... 5.3

**C**

Cade (J E) & Son Ltd, Re [1992] BCLC 213, [1991] BCC 360 .................. 5.45
Carmichael v Evans [1904] 1 Ch 486, 73 LJ Ch 329, 90 LT 573, 20 TLR 267 ..... 5.15

xx  *Table of cases*

PARA

Chez Nico (Restaurants) Ltd, Re [1992] BCLC 192 .......................... 2.46
Chichester v Chichester [1936] P 129, [1936] 1 All ER 271, 105 LJP 38, 80 Sol Jo 207, 154 LT 375, 52 TLR 265 ................................................................. 3.8
Clemens v Clemens Bros Ltd [1976] 2 All ER 268 ............................ 2.59, 5.35
Coleman v Myers [1977] 2 NZLR 225 ............................................ 2.44
Company, a, Re [1985] BCLC 80, sub nom Re a Company (No 002612 of 1984) 2 BCC 99, 263 ............................................................................. 5.52
Company, a, Re [1986] BCLC 362, sub nom Re a Company (No 007623 of 1984) 2 BCC 99, 191 ............................................................................. 5.41
Company, a, Re [1986] BCLC 376 ................................................ 5.45
Company, a (No 004475 of 1982), Re [1983] Ch 178, [1983] 2 All ER 36, [1983] 2 WLR 381, [1983] BCLC 126, 127 Sol Jo 153 ................................. 5.45
Company, a (No 008699 of 1985), Re [1986] BCLC 382, 2 BCC 24, [1986] PCC 296: 5.46
Company, a (No 004377 of 1986), Re [1987] 1 WLR 102, [1987] BCLC 94, 131 Sol Jo 132, [1987] LS Gaz R 653, sub nom Re XYZ Ltd 2 BCC 99, 520, [1987] PCC 92 ............................................................................................ 5.41
Company, a (No 005136 of 1986), Re [1987] BCLC 82, sub nom Re Sherborne Park Residents Co Ltd 2 BCC 99, 528 .................................................. 5.37
Company, a (No 004415 of 1996), Re [1997] 1 BCLC 479 ................. 5.48
Const v Harris (1824) 37 ER 1191, [1824] 34 All ER Rep 311 ............ 5.20
Consumer and Industrial Press Ltd (No 2), Re (1987) 4 BCC 72 ......... 6.54
Cook v Deeks [1916] 1 AC 554, 85 LJPC 161, [1916-17] All ER Rep 285, 114 LT 636, PC ............................................................................................ 5.33
Croftbell Ltd, Re [1990] BCLC 844, [1990] BCC 781 ....................... 6.52
Cumana Ltd, Re [1986] BCLC 430, CA .......................................... 5.48
Cutbush v Cutbush (1839) 1 Beav 184, 8 LJ Ch 175, 3 Jur 142 ........... 4.17

**D**

Daniels v Daniels [1978] Ch 406, [1978] 2 All ER 89, [1978] 2 WLR 73, 121 Sol Jo 605 .......................................................................................... 5.34
Dawnay, Day & Co Ltd v de Braconier d'Alphen [1997] IRLR 442, [1997] 26 LS Gaz R 30, 141 Sol Jo LB 129, CA ..................................................... 1.32
Diamond Fuel Co, Re (1879) 13 Ch D 400, 49 LJ Ch 301, 28 WR 309, 41 LT 573, CA ........................................................................................... 6.74
Doe d Warn v Horn (1838) 3 M & W 333 ...................................... 5.20

**E**

Ebrahimi v Westbourne Galleries Ltd [1973] AC 360, [1972] 2 All ER 492, [1972] 2 WLR 1289, 116 Sol Jo 412, HL ................... 5.23, 5.32, 5.35, 5.36, 5.45, 5.51
Edwards v Halliwell [1950] 2 All ER 1064, 94 Sol Jo 803, CA ............ 5.37
Egerton v Egerton [1949] 2 All ER 238, [1949] LJR 1683, 93 Sol Jo 551, 65 TLR 615, CA ........................................................................................... 3.44
Eley v Positive Government Security Life Assurance Co Ltd (1876) 1 Ex D 88, CA .. 5.45
Elgindata Ltd, Re [1991] BCLC 959; revsd sub nom Elgindata Ltd (No 2), Re [1993] 1 All ER 232, [1992] 1 WLR 1207, [1993] BCLC 119, [1992] 27 LS Gaz R 33, 136 Sol Jo LB 190, CA ..................................................... 2.39, 5.47
Estmanco (Kilner House) Ltd v Greater London Council [1982] 1 All ER 437, [1982] 1 WLR 2, 80 LGR 464, 125 Sol Jo 790 ........................................... 5.35

**F**

Farrow's Bank Ltd, Re [1921] 2 Ch 164, 90 LJ Ch 465, [1921] All ER Rep 511, 65 Sol Jo 679, 125 LT 699, 37 TLR 847, CA ............................................ 6.74
Ferranti International plc, Re [1994] 4 All ER 300, [1994] 2 BCLC 760, [1994] BCC 658, [1994] NLJR 1311, sub nom Talbot v Grundy [1995] 2 WLR 312; varied [1995] 2 AC 394, [1995] 2 WLR 312, [1995] ICR 1100, [1995] BCC 319, [1995] 17 LS Gaz R 47, sub nom Ferranti International plc, Re [1995] 2 All ER 65, [1995] 1 BCLC 386, [1995] NLJR 449, HL ........................................ 6.57
Fisher, Re, Harris v Fisher [1943] Ch 377, [1943] 2 All ER 615, 113 LJ Ch 17, 87 Sol Jo 372, 169 LT 289, 59 TLR 446 .................................................. 4.32

|  | PARA |
|---|---|
| Floydd v Cheney [1970] Ch 602, [1970] 1 All ER 446, [1970] 2 WLR 314, 114 Sol Jo 70 | 5.21 |
| Forte (Charles) Investments Ltd v Amanda [1964] Ch 240, [1963] 2 All ER 940, [1963] 3 WLR 662, 107 Sol Jo 494, CA | 2.61 |
| Foss v Harbottle (1843) 2 Hare 461, 67 ER 189 | 5.31 |
| Foster v Foster [1916] 1 Ch 532, 85 LJ Ch 305, [1916-17] All ER Rep 856, 114 LT 405 | 2.37 |
| Franklin and Swathling's Arbitration, Re [1929] 1 Ch 238, 98 LJ Ch 101, 140 LT 403 | 5.3 |
| Freevale Ltd v Metrostore (Holdings) Ltd [1984] Ch 199, [1984] 1 All ER 495, [1984] 2 WLR 496, 47 P & CR 481, [1984] BCLC 72, 128 Sol Jo 116 | 6.47 |
| Frith, Re, Newton v Rolfe [1902] 1 Ch 342, 71 LJ Ch 199, 86 LT 212 | 4.17 |
| Fulham Football Club Ltd v Cabra Estates plc (1992) 65 P & CR 284, [1994] 1 BCLC 363, [1992] BCC 863, CA | 2.34 |

## G

|  |  |
|---|---|
| Gaiman v National Association for Mental Health [1971] Ch 317, [1970] 2 All ER 362, [1970] 3 WLR 42, 114 Sol Jo 416 | 2.41 |
| Garland, ex p (1804) 1 Smith KB 220, 10 Ves 110, [1803-13] All ER Rep 750 | 4.16 |
| Garner v Murray [1904] 1 Ch 57, 73 LJ Ch 66, 52 WR 208, 48 Sol Jo 51, 89 LT 665 | 3.82 |
| Garwood's Trusts, Re, Garwood v Paynter [1903] 1 Ch 236, 72 LJ Ch 208, 51 WR 185, 47 Sol Jo 147 | 3.34 |
| Gordon's Will Trusts, Re, National Westminster Bank Ltd v Gordon [1978] Ch 145, [1978] 2 All ER 969, [1978] 2 WLR 754, 122 Sol Jo 148, CA | 4.29 |
| Gramophone and Typewriter Ltd v Stanley (Surveyor of Taxes) [1908] 2 KB 89, 77 LJKB 834, 15 Mans 251, [1908-10] All ER Rep 833, 99 LT 39, 24 TLR 480, sub nom Stanley (Surveyor of Taxes) v Gramophone and Typewriter Ltd 5 TC 358, CA | 2.35 |
| Green v Howell [1910] 1 Ch 495, 79 LJ Ch 549, 102 LT 347, CA | 5.13 |
| Griffiths v Secretary of State for Social Services [1974] QB 468, [1973] 3 All ER 1184, [1973] 3 WLR 831, 117 Sol Jo 873 | 6.47 |

## H

|  |  |
|---|---|
| Hall v Hall (1855) 20 Beav 139 | 5.17 |
| Halt Garage (1964) Ltd, Re [1982] 3 All ER 1016 | 1.8 |
| Harding v Glover (1810) 18 Ves 281 | 5.20 |
| Harmer (HR) Ltd, Re [1958] 3 All ER 689, [1959] 1 WLR 62, 103 Sol Jo 73, CA | 5.49 |
| Harris v A Harris Ltd 1936 SC 183, 1936 SLT 227 | 2.49 |
| Harrison v Tennant (1856) 21 Beav 482 | 5.23 |
| Hawkins v Hawkins (1858) 4 Jur NS 1044, 32 LTOS 79 | 5.17 |
| Heathcote v Hulme (1819) 1 Jac & W 122, 20 RR 245 | 4.23 |
| Highley v Walker (1910) 26 TLR 685 | 5.6 |
| Hills v M'Rae (1851) 9 Hare 297, 20 LJ Ch 533, 15 Jur 766, 17 LTOS 242 | 4.13 |
| Hitchman v Crouch Butler Savage Associates (1983) 127 Sol Jo 441, 80 LS Gaz R 554, CA | 5.12 |
| Hogg v Cramphorn Ltd [1967] Ch 254, [1966] 3 All ER 420, [1966] 3 WLR 995, 110 Sol Jo 887 | 2.40 |
| Howe v Earl of Dartmouth (1802) 6 RR 96, 7 Ves 137, 1 White & Tud LC 68, [1775-1802] All ER Rep 24 | 4.32 |

## I

|  |  |
|---|---|
| Ibbotson v Elam (1865) LR 1 Eq 188, 35 Beav 594, 12 Jur NS 114, 14 WR 241, [1861-73] All ER Rep 817 | 4.33 |

## J

|  |  |
|---|---|
| Jones v Jones [1971] 3 All ER 1201, 115 Sol Jo 869, CA | 3.41 |

## K

| | PARA |
|---|---|
| Kerr v Morris [1987] Ch 90, [1986] 3 All ER 217, [1986] 3 WLR 662, 130 Sol Jo 665, [1986] LS Gaz R 2570, CA | 5.14 |
| Kirkman v Booth (1848) 11 Beav 273, 18 LJ Ch 25, 13 Jur 525, 83 RR 158, 13 LTOS 482 | 4.15 |

## L

| | |
|---|---|
| Law v Law [1905] 1 Ch 140, 74 LJ Ch 169, 53 WR 227, [1904-7] All ER Rep 526, 49 Sol Jo 118, 92 LT 1, 21 TLR 102, CA | 5.4 |
| Lawes-Wittewronge, Re, Maurice v Bennett [1915] 1 Ch 408, 84 LJ Ch 472, [1914-15] All ER Rep 502, 112 LT 931 | 4.28 |
| Lee v Chou Wen Hsien [1984] 1 WLR 1202, [1985] BCLC 45, 128 Sol Jo 737, [1984] LS Gaz R 2929, PC | 2.40 |
| Littlewood v Caldwell (1822) 11 Price 97 | 5.18 |
| Lloyds Bank plc v Duker [1987] 3 All ER 193, [1987] 1 WLR 1324, 131 Sol Jo 1358, [1987] LS Gaz R 3254 | 4.5 |
| Loch v John Blackwood Ltd [1924] AC 783, 93 LJPC 257, [1924] B & CR 209, [1924] All ER Rep 200, 68 Sol Jo 735, 131 LT 719, 40 TLR 732, PC | 5.51 |
| London School of Electronics Ltd, Re [1986] Ch 211, [1985] 3 WLR 474, [1985] BCLC 273, 129 Sol Jo 573 | 5.43 |

## M

| | |
|---|---|
| Macaura v Northern Assurance Co Ltd [1925] AC 619, 94 LJPC 154, 31 Com Cas 10, [1925] All ER Rep 51, 69 Sol Jo 777, 133 LT 152, 41 TLR 447, HL | 1.21 |
| M'Lure v Ripley (1850) 2 Mac & G 274, sub nom M'Clure v Ripley 15 LTOS 41 | 2.14 |
| Maddeford v Austwick (1826) 1 Sim 89; affd (1833) 2 My & K 279 | 5.4 |
| Marshall v Broadhurst (1831) 1 Cr & J 403, 9 LJOS Ex 105, 1 Tyr 348 | 4.15 |
| Martin v Martin [1976] Fam 335, [1976] 3 All ER 625, [1976] 3 WLR 580, 6 Fam Law 246, 120 Sol Jo 503, CA | 3.41 |
| Menier v Hooper's Telegraph Works (1874) 9 Ch App 350, 43 LJ Ch 330, 22 WR 396, 30 LT 209, [1874-80] All ER Rep Ext 2032, CA | 5.33 |

## N

| | |
|---|---|
| National Funds Assurance Co, Re (1878) 10 Ch D 118, 48 LJ Ch 163, 27 WR 302, 39 LT 420 | 6.93 |
| New Bullas Trading Ltd, Re [1994] 1 BCLC 485, [1994] BCC 36, 12 ACLC 3203, CA: | 6.39 |
| New Zealand Banking Group v Richardson [1980] Qd R 321 | 1.25 |
| Newhart Developments Ltd v Co-operative Commercial Bank Ltd [1978] QB 814, [1978] 2 All ER 896, [1978] 2 WLR 636, 121 Sol Jo 847, CA | 6.42 |
| Newton v Newton [1989] FCR 521, [1990] 1 FLR 33, [1990] Fam Law 25, CA | 3.41 |
| North-West Transportation Co Ltd and Beatty v Beatty (1887) 12 App Cas 589, 56 LJPC 102, 36 WR 647, 57 LT 426, 3 TLR 789, PC | 2.48 |
| Nurcombe v Nurcombe [1985] 1 All ER 65, [1985] 1 WLR 370, [1984] BCLC 557, 128 Sol Jo 766, CA | 3.37 |

## P

| | |
|---|---|
| P v P [1978] 3 All ER 70, [1978] 1 WLR 483, 122 Sol Jo 230, CA | 3.41 |
| Paramount Airways Ltd (No 3), Re [1994] BCC 172, CA | 6.47 |
| Patrick and Lyon Ltd, Re [1933] Ch 786, 102 LJ Ch 300, [1933] B & CR 151, [1933] All ER Rep 590, 77 Sol Jo 250, 149 LT 231, 49 TLR 372 | 6.89 |
| Pavlides v Jensen [1956] Ch 565, [1956] 2 All ER 518, [1956] 3 WLR 224, 100 Sol Jo 452 | 5.34 |
| Peacock v Peacock (1809) 16 Ves 49 | 2.2 |
| Pender v Lushington (1877) 6 Ch D 70, 46 LJ Ch 317 | 2.48, 5.36 |
| Percival v Wright [1902] 2 Ch 421, 71 LJ Ch 846, 9 Mans 443, 51 WR 31, 46 Sol Jo 616, 18 TLR 697 | 2.43 |
| Peyton v Mindham [1971] 3 All ER 1215, [1972] 1 WLR 8, 115 Sol Jo 912 | 5.13 |

|  | PARA |
|---|---|
| Poon v Poon [1994] 2 FCR 777, [1994] 2 FLR 857 | 1.1, 3.36 |
| Posgate & Denby (Agencies) Ltd, Re [1987] BCLC 8, 2 BCC 99, 352 | 5.45 |
| Prudential Assurance Co Ltd v Newman Industries Ltd (No 2) [1981] Ch 257, [1980] 2 All ER 841, [1980] 3 WLR 543, 124 Sol Jo 756; revsd [1982] Ch 204, [1982] 1 All ER 354, [1982] 2 WLR 31, 126 Sol Jo 32, CA | 5.32, 5.36 |

### R

|  |  |
|---|---|
| Regal (Hastings) Ltd v Gulliver (1942) [1967] 2 AC 134n, [1942] 1 All ER 378, HL: | 2.42 |
| Reid v Explosives Co Ltd (1887) 19 QBD 264, 56 LJQB 388, 35 WR 509, [1886-90] All ER Rep 712, 57 LT 439, 3 TLR 588, CA | 6.47 |
| Reilly v Walsh (1848) 11 I Eq R 22 | 2.14 |
| Rhagg, Re, Easten v Boyd [1938] Ch 828, [1938] 3 All ER 314, 107 LJ Ch 436, 82 Sol Jo 546, 159 LT 434, 54 TLR 990 | 4.27, 4.29 |
| Robertson v Quiddington (1860) 28 Beav 529 | 4.28 |
| Rudd & Son Ltd, Re [1984] Ch 237, [1984] 3 All ER 225, [1984] 2 WLR 831, [1984] BCLC 279, 128 Sol Jo 330, [1984] LS Gaz R 1604; on appeal [1991] BCLC 378n, 2 BCC 98, 955, CA | 6.15 |
| Russell v Northern Bank Development Corpn Ltd [1992] 3 All ER 161, [1992] 1 WLR 588, [1992] BCLC 1016, [1992] BCC 578, [1992] 27 LS Gaz R 33, 136 Sol Jo LB 182, HL | 2.64, 5.53 |

### S

|  |  |
|---|---|
| Salmon v Quin & Axtens Ltd [1909] 1 Ch 311, 78 LJ Ch 367, 16 Mans 127, 53 Sol Jo 150, 100 LT 161, 25 TLR 164, CA; affd sub nom Quin & Axtens Ltd v Salmon [1909] AC 442, 78 LJ Ch 506, 16 Mans 230, 53 Sol Jo 575, 100 LT 820, 25 TLR 590, HL | 2.36 |
| Salomon v A Salomon & Co Ltd [1897] AC 22, 66 LJ Ch 35, 4 Mans 89, 45 WR 193, [1895-9] All ER Rep 33, 41 Sol Jo 63, 75 LT 426, 13 TLR 46, HL | 1.4, 6.1, 6.96 |
| Scarf v Jardine (1882) 7 App Cas 345, 51 LJQB 612, 30 WR 893, [1881-5] All ER Rep 651, 47 LT 258, HL | 3.72 |
| Scottish Co-operative Wholesale Society Ltd v Meyer [1959] AC 324, [1958] 3 All ER 66, [1958] 3 WLR 404, 102 Sol Jo 617, 1958 SC (HL) 40, HL | 5.47 |
| Sheppard v Oxenford (1855) 1 K & J 491, 3 WR 384, 25 LTOS 63; on appeal (1855) 1 K & J 501n, 3 WR 397, 25 LTOS 90, CA | 5.20 |
| Siebe Gorman & Co Ltd v Barclays Bank Ltd [1979] 2 Lloyd's Rep 142 | 6.39 |
| Simpson v Chapman (1853) 4 De GM & G 154 | 4.26 |
| Smith (Howard) Ltd v Ampol Petroleum Ltd [1974] AC 821, [1974] 1 All ER 1126, [1974] 2 WLR 689, 118 Sol Jo 330, PC | 2.37 |
| Smith & Fawcett Ltd, Re [1942] Ch 304, [1942] 1 All ER 542, 111 LJ Ch 265, 86 Sol Jo 147, 166 LT 279, CA | 2.40, 2.60 |
| Solicitors' Arbitration, A, Re [1962] 1 All ER 772, [1962] 1 WLR 353, 106 Sol Jo 221: | 5.13 |
| Strickland v Symons (1884) 26 Ch D 245, 53 LJ Ch 582, 32 WR 889, 51 LT 406, CA | 4.17 |
| Stroud v Gwyer (1860) 28 Beav 130, 6 Jur NS 719, 126 RR 57, 2 LT 400 | 4.21 |
| Swaledale Cleaners Ltd, Re [1968] 3 All ER 619, [1968] 1 WLR 1710, 112 Sol Jo 781, CA | 2.60 |

### T

|  |  |
|---|---|
| Trench Tubeless Tyre Co, Re, Bethell v Trench Tubeless Tyre Co [1900] 1 Ch 408, 69 LJ Ch 213, 8 Mans 85, 48 WR 310, 44 Sol Jo 260, 82 LT 247, 16 TLR 207, CA: | 3.54 |
| Trollope's Will Trusts, Re, Public Trustee v Trollope [1927] 1 Ch 596, 96 LJ Ch 340, [1927] All ER Rep 365, 71 Sol Jo 310, 137 LT 375 | 4.32 |
| Turner v Turner [1911] 1 Ch 716, 80 LJ Ch 473, [1911-13] All ER Rep 962, 104 LT 901, CA | 4.30 |

### U

|  |  |
|---|---|
| Unisoft Group Ltd (No 3), Re [1994] 1 BCLC 609, [1994] BCC 766 | 5.39 |
| Upton v Brown (1884) 26 Ch D 588, 54 LJ Ch 614, 32 WR 679, 51 LT 591 | 4.32 |

## V

Vyse v Foster (1872) 8 Ch App 309, 42 LJ Ch 245, 21 WR 207, 27 LT 774; affd (1874) LR 7 HL 318, 44 LJ Ch 37, 23 WR 355, 31 LT 177 .................. 4.21, 4.23, 4.25

## W

Walker v Hirsch (1884) 27 Ch D 460, 54 LJ Ch 315, 32 WR 992, 51 LT 481, CA ... 5.17
Walters v Bingham [1988] 1 FTLR 260, [1988] NLJR 7 ..................... 3.75, 5.12
Weiner's Will Trusts, Re, Wyner v Braithwaite [1956] 2 All ER 482, [1956] 1 WLR 579, 100 Sol Jo 400 ....................................................... 4.5
Weller (Sam) & Sons Ltd, Re [1990] Ch 682, [1989] 3 WLR 923, [1990] BCLC 80, 5 BCC 810 ............................................................ 5.48
Wightman v Townroe (1813) 1 M & S 412, 14 RR 475 ...................... 4.15
Wilkinson v Henderson (1833) 1 My & K 582, 2 LJ Ch 190 .................. 4.13
Wood v Scoles (1866) 1 Ch App 369, 35 LJ Ch 547, 12 Jur NS 555, 14 WR 621, 14 LT 470 ................................................................. 3.81

## Y

Yenidje Tobacco Co Ltd, Re [1916] 2 Ch 426, 86 LJ Ch 1, [1916] HBR 140, [1916-17] All ER Rep 1050, 60 Sol Jo 707, 115 LT 530, 32 TLR 709, CA ........ 3.73, 5.23, 5.51

Chapter 1

# Formation of a business – partnership or company?

INTRODUCTION

**1.1** The concept of the family business defies an accurate legal definition.[1] For the purposes of this book, the family business may be defined as a business enterprise operated by individuals who are related by blood or marriage, usually encompassing more than one generation. In many instances the family business may be the main, or only family asset. Fiscal considerations, the obtaining of finance, or ease of management of the enterprise may determine whether the family business is to be run as a partnership under the provisions of the Partnership Act 1890,[2] or as a private limited company registered under the Companies Act 1985.

1 Nevertheless the concept has long been recognised by the courts, both within the context of the partnership and the private limited company. See the comments of Thorpe J in the case of *Poon v Poon* [1994] 2 FCR 777, [1994] 2 FLR 857.
2 This book will not consider the limited partnership the operation of which is principally governed by the Limited Partnerships Act 1907. This form of business enterprise is rarely encountered in England and Wales.

**1.2** It is difficult to calculate the prevalence of the family business in England and Wales, this is in part because there is no agreed definition of a family business. Nevertheless, according to the Department of Trade and Industry, over 75% of businesses operating in England and Wales are family enterprises.[1] This book will consider some of the problems that may be faced by the family business, and the possible advantages and disadvantages of operating the enterprise either as a partnership or a private limited company.

1 See also 'The Survey of the Stoy Centre For Family Businesses' from the Warwick Business School.

**1.3** In this introductory chapter, an outline will be given of some of the issues that may be considered by a family business from its inception and during its operation, and which may determine whether the business should or should not be incorporated.

LIMITED LIABILITY

**1.4** It is received wisdom that the principal advantage in operating a family business as a private limited company is that its members as shareholders are protected from personal bankruptcy, their liability to the enterprise is limited only to the extent that the shares in the company are not fully paid up.[1] It is the company as a separate legal entity which is liable without limit for the liabilities and debts of the business.[2] By way of contrast, the partnership is an enterprise which is in no way distinct from its members or partners. Even when the partnership operates behind a business name, it remains no more than the joint and common enterprise of the partners. The assets of the partnership as well as the private or separate estates of each of the partners are liable to satisfy the debts and liabilities of the business without limit.

1 This is a rare event in the modern private limited company as virtually all shares are issued to the shareholders fully paid up.
2 It is therefore strictly inaccurate to call the company a limited enterprise. It is liable to the full extent of its assets, the limited liability is that of the shareholders. The legal reality and consequences of limited liability were examined in the leading case of *Salomon v A Salomon & Co Ltd* [1897] AC 22, HL.

**1.5** Despite the above, the reality behind these legal forms of business is frequently different. The family private company may need to borrow money in order to prosper or even to survive. Financial institutions may require guarantees in order to supply the required finance. The parties who will supply these guarantees will invariably be the directors/shareholders of the company.[1] The effect of these guarantees will be that the failure of the business will render the company insolvent,[2] and the directors/shareholders will suffer personal bankruptcy.[3] In these cases, the limited liability of the director/shareholder is a fiction.

1 In the case of the family company the directors of the company will be the principal or only shareholders, hence the use of the term director/shareholder.
2 See Chapter 6 for a consideration of the insolvency procedures applicable to a private limited company.
3 The same situation occurs if the financial institutions insist that the directors/shareholders give security over their personal assets as a condition of the company receiving financial aid.

FINANCING THE BUSINESS

**1.6** As mentioned above, institutional lenders, who are the usual source of finance for the family business will require security for any financial advances made to a business enterprise. A particularly effective form of security for the institutional lender is the floating charge.[1] In most instances, a company will grant both a floating and fixed charge over its assets. This form of charge is known as a composite charge. Many institutional lenders favour the floating charge as being a particularly effective security, and are willing to lend only on the basis that the business can create such a charge over its business assets. The private limited company is capable of granting a floating charge over its assets, but the partnership cannot grant such a security over its assets. The consequence of this restriction is that a family business may be forced to incorporate, in order to raise finance.

1 For the nature of a floating charge, see Chapter 6, para 6.39, n 53.

FISCAL ADVANTAGES

**1.7** In many private limited companies including the family company, the directors constitute all the shareholders with a right to remuneration calculated in proportion to their shareholding. In these cases, it may be more tax efficient[1] to distribute any profits of the business by way of dividend and not by way of director remuneration. When a distribution is made by a company resident in the United Kingdom, the recipient is assessable to income tax under Schedule F.[2] At present, if the distribution is a 'qualifying distribution', advance corporation tax is payable at that time.[3] Distributions whether qualifying or not, are not deductible in computing the profits of the company.[4] However, the payment of a dividend will not, unlike the payment of remuneration, attract liability to make either primary or secondary national insurance contributions. This is a tax saving when compared to a distribution made by a partnership to its partners, which will be subject to national insurance contributions. Nevertheless with current rates of corporation tax and higher rate income tax roughly comparable,[5] the tax advantages of incorporation are not significant enough to justify incorporation solely on this ground.

1 And therefore constitute a reason for incorporation of the business as opposed to operating the enterprise as a partnership.
2 Income and Corporation Taxes Act 1988, s 20.
3 Although the Chancellor of the Exchequer announced in his November 1997 statement that advance corporation tax will be abolished from April 1999.
4 Income and Corporation Taxes Act 1988, s 337(2).
5 This remains broadly true notwithstanding the lower rate of corporation tax for companies which have profits which do not exceed £300,000, see s 13 of the Income and Corporation Taxes Act 1988, and that dividends are currently taxed at 20%. Regard should also be had to marginal relief whereby a company whose profits are more than £300,000 but less than £1.5 million will pay corporation tax at less than the standard rate on a sliding scale up to the full rate as the profits of the company achieves and then exceeds the latter sum. For a full consideration of both corporation tax and income tax as applicable to businesses see *Tiley & Collison's UK Tax Guide 1997–1998* published by Butterworths.

**1.8** Furthermore, in many family companies, the distribution of profits may be dictated by fiscal considerations, namely tax avoidance. In the case of *Re Halt Garage (1964) Ltd*,[1] Oliver J concluded that in the absence of fraud, the company had the power to distribute profits in any way that proved tax efficient.[2]

1 [1982] 3 All ER 1016 at 1033.
2 In the instant case, it was at that time more tax efficient to distribute profits by way of directors' remuneration. The case therefore illustrates that the tax regime is subject to constant change, and future fiscal legislation may establish a clear advantage in favour of incorporation of a family business.

COMPARATIVE COSTS OF OPERATING A FAMILY BUSINESS

**1.9** It is an axiom of operating a business that administrative costs should be kept to a minimum. In this regard, the partnership is perceived as having certain advantages over a private limited company. The lack of formal legal requirements to file documents such as articles of association and the memorandum of association are perceived to give the partnership both cost and administrative advantages over the company as a business medium. Nevertheless, the preparation of a comprehensive and well-drafted partnership agreement will incur costs that are at least equal to the costs of setting up a private limited company, even where the company is an 'off the shelf' company. However, the setting up of a company may require the preparation of a shareholder agreement,[1] the costs of which should equal that of a well-drafted partnership agreement.

[1] The nature form and uses of such a document are considered in Chapter 2, para 2.63 onwards.

## Accounts

**1.10** In general, there is no specific legal requirement for partnerships to keep accounts.[1] Nevertheless, no well-run business could survive without the keeping of accounts, furthermore a partnership's tax liabilities are effectively calculated by recourse to accounts. In addition, s 28 of the Partnership Act 1890 imposes on partners an obligation to render true accounts, and full information of all things affecting the partnership. Accordingly, the costs of keeping accounts is a necessary expense of running the business.

[1] Ie there is no direct legal sanction if the partnership fails to keep accounts.

**1.11** The statutory requirement on the directors of the company to prepare a balance sheet and a profit and loss account,[1] together with a report on such matters, must be regarded in the light of both the administration and the costs of running a business. These documents, together with an annual auditor's report must be filed with the Registrar of Companies.[2] There is no requirement for a partnership's accounts to be filed and they can therefore be kept from public scrutiny which includes employees. This right of the partnership to keep its accounts, which includes private is an advantage in running a business as an unincorporated enterprise, although this matter must be considered in the context of the rather de-regulated regime of filing company accounts that can be applied to the private limited company, and which are considered in outline below.

[1] Companies Act 1985, s 226.
[2] Ibid s 242(1).

### EXEMPTIONS AND EXCEPTIONS TO THE ACCOUNTING REQUIREMENTS

**1.12** There are a number of exemptions and exceptions available to a private limited company and therefore the family company, which allow such an enterprise to evade, to a greater or lesser degree,[1] the accounting requirements which were considered above. The principal exemptions applicable to the family company are those applicable to the small or medium-sized company.

[1] For a more comprehensive consideration of the accounting requirements generally applicable to private limited companies, see Prime & Scanlan *The Law of Private Limited Companies* (Butterworths, 1995 Chapter 15).

## Small and medium-sized companies

**1.13** The major requirement of a company relating to public disclosure of its financial position is the filing of its accounts with the Registrar of Companies. The statutory requirements governing the extent of disclosure of financial information in the accounts are extensive and detailed. However, the directors of small and medium-sized[1] private companies may, if they wish, deliver abbreviated accounts and reports, thereby keeping some details of the company's affairs private, as in the case of a partnership. The extent to which a company may depart from the stringent statutory requirements of disclosure of the company's financial affairs depends on whether the company satisfies the condition of being either a small or medium-sized company.

1 For a definition of these terms see para 1.14 below.

**1.14** A company must qualify as a small or medium-sized company on an annual basis in order to qualify for full or partial exemption from the statutory requirements relating to company accounts. A company qualifies as small or medium-sized in any given financial year if it satisfies certain conditions in relation to both that year and the preceding year, unless it is the company's first financial year, when the conditions have to be satisfied for that financial year alone.[1] In order to qualify as a small company, the turnover must not be more than £2.8 million, its balance sheet not more than £1.4 million in total, and it must not employ more than 50 people.[2] A company qualifies as medium-sized along similar lines if its turnover is not more than £11.2 million, its balance sheet total does not exceed £5.6 million, and it does not employ more than 250 people.[2] Many family companies will therefore qualify as either small or medium-sized.

1 Companies Act 1985, s 247(1).
2 Section 247(2) and (3) and SI 1992/2452, reg 5.

**1.15** Once a company is qualified under the above rules, its directors are entitled to claim the same status in future years provided that the company satisfies the relevant conditions at least every other year, but, if the conditions are not satisfied for two consecutive years, the company cannot then qualify.[1]

1 Companies Act 1985, s 247(2).

## FORM OF ABBREVIATED ACCOUNTS AND REPORTS

### Medium-sized companies

**1.16** Where a company qualifies as a medium-sized company, the directors have to file the normal accounts. However, certain items in the profit and loss accounts may be combined as one item under the heading 'gross profit or loss'. If the company has carried on two or more classes of substantially different business, then there is no reason to break down the turnover and to attribute it to each type of business.[1]

1 Which is a normal requirement of the Companies Act 1985, Sch 4, para 55.

### Small companies

**1.17** Where a company qualifies as a small company, then the directors are permitted to prepare an abbreviated balance sheet and have to file neither their profit and loss accounts[1] nor their directors' report.[2] They are also allowed to file an abbreviated balance sheet.[3]

1 Companies Act 1985, Sch 8, Pt II, para 18.
2 Ibid Sch 8, Pt II, para 20.
3 Ibid para 39.

### Dispensing with laying accounts

**1.18** Since the Companies Act of 1989,[1] private limited companies have had the power to dispense with the holding of annual general meetings. In support of this, a regime was created to allow private limited companies to elect to dispense with the laying of accounts and reports before any such meetings.[2] Without such a provision, it would have been necessary for an annual general meeting to be held simply to go through the formality of approving accounts. If a company elects to dispense with the laying of accounts, it must then circulate the accounts and reports to all those entitled to attend the general meeting, which then only takes place if a shareholder or the auditors indicate that they require a meeting for the purposes of discussing the accounts.

1 Section 115, inserting s 366A of the Companies Act 1985.
2 Section 379A. Such an election is only likely to be made if there has also been an election to dispense with the holding of annual general meetings under s 366A.

COMPANY AUDITORS

**1.19** Every family company is required to appoint an auditor. The auditor's report provides an independent review of the financial affairs of the company and will enable members of the company to determine whether proper accounting records have been kept by the company. However, the Companies Act 1985 (Audit Exemption) Regulations[1] provide for small companies, including family companies, to be exempted from the normal auditing requirements for companies, provided that they meet the conditions for exemption.[2]

1 SI 1994/1935 as amended by SI 1994/2879.
2 Space does not permit a consideration of these requirements. For a more detailed review see Prime & Scanlan *The Law of Private Limited Companies*, Chapter 15.

### Conclusion

**1.20** The new regime for deregulation and possible dispensation with the statutory requirements relating to the preparation and filing of company accounts enables the vast majority of family companies to save the time and costs of preparing the company accounts. The new regime is not therefore radically different from the way in which a well-run family partnership may both prepare its accounts and disseminate the relevant information to its members. Furthermore, the new regime enables a family company to preserve some of the information on its financial affairs from public scrutiny. Prior to the introduction of this new regime, the requirement for all companies to prepare and file highly detailed accounts was perceived as a disincentive to incorporating a family business, both from the point of view of the administrative costs and public disclosure. This is no longer the case and the family company can, at least as regards business accounts, be run along similar lines to a family partnership.

## INCORPORATION

**1.21** The very fact that a company is a legal entity as distinct from that of its members is a cogent reason for operating a family business as a private limited company.[1] Unlike a partnership, the assets of the business can be vested in the company without formality.[2] In the case of a partnership, it is of prime importance to distinguish between partnership property and property used by the partnership which remains the exclusive property of one of the partners. Furthermore, since the partnership has no legal existence, it cannot hold property. Accordingly, property which is intended to be used by the partnership must be vested in the partners jointly as trustees for themselves, although the property will generally be held beneficially in common. The holding of partnership property in trust by all or some of the partners is not an insurmountable difficulty, although where there are more than four partners, any real property which the partners intend as partnership property cannot be vested in more than four of the partners as joint tenants.[3] The death of one or more of these partners will require the vesting of the property in new partners/trustees.

1 See in particular Chapters 3 and 4 concerning the family business on the divorce and/or death of a member of the family business.
2 Although this matter should be noted when issues of insurance of business assets are considered together with the parties who can be said to have an insurable interest in the business assets. See *Macaura v Northern Assurance Co Ltd* [1925] AC 619, HL.
3 Law of Property Act 1925, s 34(2).

### Selling of business in whole or in part

**1.22** The building up of the family business may result in the need to acquire finance from sources other than borrowing. The finance needed to expand the business into new areas may be financed by selling part of the current business to third parties. Furthermore, the death of a member of the family business, or marital discord within the business, may lead the members or surviving members of the enterprise to sell the business as a going concern. In such cases, the company has significant advantages over the partnership. The legal aspects of the sale are relatively free from legal problems irrespective of whether the sale is effected by the transfer of the assets of the company, or by transfer of the shares in the enterprise. A family enterprise which is a partnership may be incorporated in order to carry out a sale of the business.

## HIVING OFF PARTS OF A BUSINESS

**1.23** Even a family business may, as a consequence of growth and success, seek to diversify its activities. Various aspects of the business may need to be run and administered as separate if not independent enterprises.[1] In such cases, the private limited company is the most efficient and appropriate business organisation to achieve these objectives. Each part of the family's business may be operated through the medium of a nominally independent private limited company, with the respective companies enjoying common shareholders. Alternatively, the original family company may also operate as a holding company of the subsidiary family companies which operate the various parts of the collective family business.

1 This may be even more important where one aspect of the business is financially a risk and the availability of limited liability cannot be discounted.

**1.24** Where the partners in a family partnership wish to diversify their business activities, they may hive off aspects of their business by means of a sub-partnership. A sub-partnership is, in essence, a partnership within a partnership. Such an enterprise, although it constitutes a share in another partnership, and is derived from the latter which is generally defined as the principal partnership, nevertheless operates outside the confines of the principal partnership. Any agreement to share the profits of a sub-partnership will bring about a partnership only between those who are a party to the sub-partnership agreement.

**1.25** In the case of *Bray v Fromont*,[1] the court emphasised the point that partners who are solely partners in the respective sub-partnership[2] and principal partnership are not thereby constituted as partners inter se. It has been held in the Australian case of *New Zealand Banking Group v Richardson*[3] that a sub-partner could not be fully responsible for the losses of the principal partnership. However, the sub-partner had to bear a proportion of any such losses which had to be borne by the sub-partners who were also partners in the principal partnership.

1 (1821) 6 Madd 5.
2 Or sub-partnerships.
3 [1980] Qd R 321.

**1.26** On the creation of a sub-partnership, it does not follow that any of the terms contained in the principal partnership agreement will by implication automatically be incorporated into the sub-partnership agreement, or be regarded as governing that enterprise. It follows from the above, that the sub-partnership will not necessarily endure for the same term as the principal partnership. It is for these reasons that the sub-partnership is not the most appropriate business form to operate subsidiary aspects of the main family business.

MERGERS

**1.27** For the sake of completeness, reference should be made to the possibility of a family business merging with another enterprise. Where both enterprises are companies, the merger of the enterprises may be brought about by a number of procedures. The two businesses may be transferred to a newly-formed third company, in which the respective members of the two original companies are shareholders. Alternatively, a holding company may be formed and the two companies may become subsidiaries of the holding company.

**1.28** The merging of enterprises, where the businesses are partnerships, will generally prove more problematic. In essence, the only effective way of merging the enterprises will be by forming a partnership between the two businesses. However, the 'group partnership' has certain characteristics. The partnership has no existence separate from that of its members. In the case of a group partnership, each member of each of the partnerships is also a constituent member of the group partnership. It is in essence, therefore, a single partnership. Since a group partnership consists of the collective membership of all the partners of the respective constituent partnerships, regard must be had to the general statutory restriction on the formation of partnerships of more than 20 partners.[1] Merger of businesses may therefore be more easily effected where the participants are companies.

1 Companies Act 1985, s 716(1). This restriction is relaxed in the case of partnerships which carry on certain professions. For example, partnerships of solicitors or accountants may consist of more than 20 partners.

**1.29** Certain enterprises or professions can only be carried on collectively in the form of a partnership. Thus the Law Society will not permit the profession of solicitor to be carried on collectively except within the context of a partnership.

## DISCRIMINATION AND SOCIAL WELFARE LEGISLATION

**1.30** Operating a family business, as in the case of any other enterprise, will require the participants to observe the relevant legislation. Compliance with employment and social welfare legislation may prove costly to a small business enterprise. The prime example of such legislation is anti-discrimination legislation. Whereas a company, irrespective of its size must comply with the provisions of the Race Relations Act 1976,[1] a partnership of less than six partners need not observe the Act.[2] This may be a factor for a small family business in determining whether its participants should operate the enterprise as a partnership or as a private limited company.

1 See s 1 of the Act, though the possible impact of EC legislation in this area cannot be ignored.
2 Race Relations Act 1976 s 10(1). By s 73 (ibid) the number of partners specified for the purposes of the application of the Act may be altered by an order made by the Secretary of State.

## RESTRAINT OF TRADE

**1.31** Even a family business may build up a fund of goodwill and expertise over the course of time which would prove valuable to competitors. It is crucial for the survival and continued prosperity of the business that such intellectual property is protected. Where a member of the business leaves the enterprise, he must be prevented from using such intellectual property in direct competition with his former business associates. In the case of a partnership, it is normal practice for a well-drafted partnership agreement to seek to protect the goodwill and expertise by prohibiting or restricting a former partner from carrying on a business[1] in competition with the business of the partnership. A clause in a partnership agreement should also seek to prevent an ex-partner from enticing away the partnership's customers, clients, or even employees. Because of the relationship between partners, such clauses constitute covenants between the partners as well as restraint of trade clauses, and may be enforceable if the following conditions are satisfied:

(a) any such clause must seek to protect only the legitimate business interests of the partnership; and
(b) the clause must be strictly limited in time and geographical area.[2]

1 Either alone or in partnership with others.
2 For a full consideration of restraint of trade clauses in partnership agreements see Prime & Scanlan *The Law of Partnership*, Chapter 5. For examples of such clauses see 30 *Forms & Precedents*.

**1.32** The enforceability of restraint of trade clauses between the family company and its directors/shareholders may prove more problematic than in the case of a partnership. Where a director/shareholder leaves the company, transfers his shareholding and then acts in contravention of such a clause, it is the company who would take legal action to enforce the provision. Where remaining shareholders in the family company do not wish to enforce the clause against the former member, they may be able to muster sufficient voting power to prevent the company from taking the action.[1] Since the company is a legal body independent from its shareholders, it is the company which has the legitimate interest in the enforcement of such restraint of trade clauses, and not a particular shareholder.[2] The partners in a family partnership may, however, seek to enforce such a clause in the partnership agreement, both on behalf of the partnership and on their own behalf. This may be a powerful incentive for the participants in a family business to carry on the enterprise through the medium of the partnership rather than a limited liability company.

1 There may be emotional reasons or family ties with the former director shareholder, or expected future financial benefit. See Chapters 2, para 2.48 and 5, para 5.26 where consideration is given to the power of a shareholder to vote on company issues in accordance with his own interests even though this is in conflict with the interests of the company.
2 It must be noted that doubt has been cast upon the above as a statement of principle in the recent case of *Dawnay, Day & Co Ltd v de Braconier d'Alphen* [1997] IRLR 442, CA. The case involved the enforcement of restraint of trade clauses by the shareholder of a joint venture company against a former group of shareholders. For a full consideration of the case within the context principally of a joint venture company, see Prime, Gale & Scanlan *The Law and Practice of Joint Ventures* (Butterworths, 1997). At the time of writing it is difficult to determine fully the effect of this decision and whether it is applicable only in the case of the special regime of the joint venture company.

## Conclusion

**1.33** This Chapter has considered in outline some of the factors that may be relevant to the participants in a family business, in determining whether they should operate their business either as a partnership or as a private limited company, or if they set up their enterprise as a partnership, whether they should subsequently incorporate the business. The following chapters give further consideration to the comparative advantages of operating a family business in either an incorporated or unincorporated form, where issues such as marital discord or death of the participants arise. Although the following chapters will illustrate that the differences between the operation of the partnership and the company, in the various circumstances noted in the text, are not as great as may be conceived, having regard to the different statutory rules applicable to the two business mediums; nevertheless there may be particular situations where there are considerable advantages in operating the family business in one of these business forms. The book will however, illustrate that the selection of either of these enterprises is generally a complex decision calling for careful judgment on the part of the members. It will usually be based on an assessment of a number of factors which may be in conflict with one another. Consideration will first be given to the comparative advantages of operating the family business as either a company or a partnership.

# Chapter 2

# Operating the enterprise

RUNNING THE BUSINESS – THE PARTNERSHIP

**2.1** The smooth running of the family business should be regarded as a matter of prime importance. The family partnership must provide mechanisms for determining policy, and in cases where there are disputes as to how the business is to be managed, a means of settling such disputes. These objectives can be achieved in the case of a partnership by recourse to provisions in the Partnership Act 1890, and by reference to the partnership deed or agreement. Consideration will first be given to the relevant provisions of the Partnership Act.

THE RIGHT TO PARTICIPATE IN PARTNERSHIP AFFAIRS

**2.2** Section 24(5) of the Partnership Act 1890 provides that 'every partner may take part in the management of the partnership business'. This statutory recognition of the right of every partner to participate in the management of the business of the partnership is subject to contrary provision, either express or implied, in the partnership agreement. The courts will not, however, readily exclude a partner from the right to participate in the partnership business by any other means.[1] It is therefore advisable for the partnership agreement to specify whether all or only some of the partners are to participate in the management of the business.[2] The agreement should require that the partners who are empowered to carry on the management of the partnership business should devote themselves full-time to the affairs of the partnership. This is necessary because there is no requirement either by case law or by statutory provision for a partner to devote himself exclusively to the affairs of the partnership.

1 *Peacock v Peacock* (1809) 16 Ves 49. It should be noted that any attempt to exclude a partner from the right to participate in the management of the business of the partnership on the grounds of sex or race may be unlawful.
2 See 30 *Forms & Precedents* Form 2, clause 20.

**2.3** Notwithstanding any restriction on the right of a partner to participate in the management of the partnership,[1] third parties may deal with all the members of the partnership as if they all carried equal authority to bind the business unless they have actual notice to the contrary.[2] This will be especially important for the family partnership, where the normally close relationship of the family members would suggest to a third party that a partner has power to conclude agreements on behalf of the partnership. This may not necessarily be implied in the case of a partner in a normal trading or professional partnership.

1 A sleeping or dormant partner is not usually given management rights in the day-to-day running of the partnership business. See 30 *Forms & Precedents* Form 66.
2 Partnership Act 1890, ss 5 and 8.

PARTNERSHIP DECISIONS – PARTNERSHIP AGREEMENT

**2.4** The partnership agreement (in the case of a family partnership) must provide a means for the resolution of disputes between its members. In the absence of the unanimous approval of the partners, the partnership agreement must specify the issues that may be determined by a majority of the partners rather than by unanimous agreement. In the absence of any such agreement s 24(8) of the Partnership Act 1890 provides:

> 'Any difference arising as to the ordinary matters connected with the partnership business may be decided by a majority of the partners, but no change may be made in the nature of the partnership business without the consent of all existing partners.'

**2.5** Section 24(8) is difficult to apply in practice and so a well-drafted partnership agreement should deal with the following:

**2.6** *Matters requiring the approval by the majority of the partners entitled to participate in the management of the business.*[1] This will usually include matters such as the employment and dismissal of staff. It is normal practice to provide that all management decisions may be determined by majority voting except for those specifically listed in the partnership agreement as requiring unanimous approval.[2]

1 See 30 *Forms & Precedents* Form 62.
2 See ibid Form 62.

**2.7** *Matters that will require the unanimous consent of the participating partners.* This would generally include the partnership engaging in a new form of business as distinct from that normally carried on by the partnership.

**2.8** The partnership agreement may provide that all matters relating to the management and conduct of the affairs of the partnership shall be determined by majority, subject to a veto by a named partner or partners.

**2.9** It may be advisable in the case of a family partnership for the partnership agreement to provide for the specific exclusion of named partners from all or some of the activities of management, for example in the hiring and firing of staff.

SPECIAL MAJORITIES

**2.10.** Certain matters concerning the affairs of the partnership may be decided by a special majority, usually three quarters of the votes cast if the partnership agreement so provides. Such matters generally relate to issues such as:

(a) the borrowing of money or the lending in excess of a prescribed sum,
(b) the giving of any guarantee,

(c) the opening of any branch office,
(d) the sale of one or any partnership premises; or
(e) any increase in the capital of the partnership.[1]

1 See 30 *Forms & Precedents* Form 54.

## DETERMINATION OF MAJORITY

**2.11** It has been noted above that management decisions in a family partnership will be taken by majority vote amongst the partners entitled to vote on such matters. Even in a family partnership it will not be a majority determined by the number of partners, instead it will be determined in proportion to the respective partnership shares of the net profits of the business.

## PROVISION FOR PARTNERSHIP MEETINGS

**2.12** It will usually be highly desirable that provision be made in the partnership agreement for the holding of regular partnership meetings.[1] Provision should also be made to regulate the procedure to be followed at such meetings. For instance any valid resolution relating to the affairs of the partnership, must be passed at a meeting at which the minimum prescribed notice has been given to all the partners entitled to participate in the management of the business. The partnership agreement should also prescribe a quorum for any such meetings. Provision should also be made for a participating partner to approve in writing any resolution relating to the affairs of the partnership proposed at a meeting, provided he has been given notice of the meeting.[2]

1 See 30 *Forms & Precedents* Forms 63 and 64.
2 See ibid Form 64.

## ACCOUNTS

**2.13** A family partnership, like any other partnership, is a business carried on with a view to profit.[1] The profits are therefore to be divided between its members in accordance with the terms of the partnership agreement. It would therefore be a sensible management technique to ensure that the family partnership keeps partnership accounts. The partnership agreement should also require the keeping of a balance sheet. One aspect of the keeping of accounts is to show what is due to each partner in respect of his capital invested in the business. In a family partnership, the death of a partner will generally result in the partnership share accruing to the remaining partners. This will have both inheritance tax and capital gains tax consequences.

1 See the Partnership Act 1890, s 1.

## PARTNERS' DUTIES

**2.14** It is good practice for the family partnership agreement to set out in detail the duties which the partners owe inter se, rather than relying on those prescribed by case law and the Partnership Act 1890. These duties are imposed on a partner either by law, equity or statute, the principal duty being good faith. These duties are reciprocal. Nevertheless, the breach of any such duty will not in itself release the other partners from their obligations to the partner in breach. This includes their duty to act in good faith. If a partner repeatedly commits serious breaches of his obligations to his co-partners, then they can maintain that the recalcitrant partner has repudiated the partnership. This will only release the other partners from the obligation to observe their duties as partners to the partner in breach.[1] Accordingly, the partnership agreement should prescribe which duties the partners owe inter se, and should also provide that breach of certain of these duties by a partner will give the other partners the power to expel the partner in breach.[2]

1 *M'Lure v Ripley* (1850) 2 Mac & G 274; *Reilly v Walsh* (1848) 11 I Eq R 22.
2 The breach of any of these obligations should also give rise to an action in damages for breach of covenant and may be subject to injunctive relief. The power to dissolve the partnership for persistent or extensive breaches of such obligations should also be considered. The grounds upon which a partnership may be dissolved and the nature of dissolution are considered in Chapters 3 and 5.

PRESCRIBED DUTIES

**2.15** The duties which will commonly be set out in a partnership agreement will include:

(a) a duty to be just and faithful to the other partners;
(b) a duty to disclose to the co-partners all matters relating to the partnership affairs;
(c) a duty to give full time and attention to the partnership and to employ himself diligently in its business;
(d) a duty to use his best skills and endeavours to carry on the business for the benefit of the partnership;
(e) a duty to pay his separate debts and to indemnify his co-partners from any failure to do so and
(f) a duty to account for all fees, emoluments and commissions received by him from any position held by him while a partner, except in so far as the partners may agree otherwise.

**2.16** The requirement that a partner devote his full time and attention to the affairs of the partnership should be tempered by a provision for a partner to be absent from the partnership in certain prescribed circumstances. The partnership agreement should also provide for a partner taking more than his entitlement of periods of absence by requiring an adjustment of profits.[1] The partnership agreement may also make provision preventing partners from absenting themselves at the same time as other partners are on leave.[2] In the case of family partnerships, absences of partners may arise through family events and such provisions for absences are therefore crucial.[3]

1 See ibid Form 25.
2 See ibid Form 24. The relevant clause should specify the maximum number of partners who may be absent from the partnership and this should also include married partners.
3 This will particularly be the case where a partner seeks maternity or paternity leave, see para 2.29, below.

## INDEMNITIES

**2.17** As the activities of a partner are carried out on behalf of the partnership, it is appropriate that indemnities be given among the partners in respect of damages and/or costs arising from a partner's breach of his obligations.[1]

1 See 30 *Forms & Precedents* Form 1, para 22 and Form 2, clause 7.2.

## DEATH OR RETIREMENT OF A PARTNER

**2.18** Section 33(1) of the Partnership Act 1890 provides that subject to any contrary agreement between the partners, every partnership is dissolved by the death of a partner.[1] In most family partnerships, such an occurrence would be an unfortunate and undesirable solution. Most family partnerships with a well established business with extensive goodwill are quite capable of being carried on by the surviving partners despite the death of even the founding member of the enterprise. Accordingly the partnership agreement should provide for the continuation of the firm by the surviving partners, notwithstanding the death of a partner.[2]

1 Similar provision is made with regard to the bankruptcy of a partner. The dissolution would in these cases be a general dissolution bringing the partnership to an end. See Chapters 3 and 5 and Prime & Scanlan *The Law of Partnership*, Chapter 12.
2 The agreement should therefore provide that the death of the partner constitutes a technical dissolution of the partnership. In such cases the partnership continues with the surviving members constituting a new partnership.

**2.19** The dependants of a deceased partner, or those beneficiaries entitled under the deceased partner's will[1] may claim the deceased partner's share in the partnership.[2] The partnership agreement should therefore provide how the value of the deceased partner's share of the partnership assets is to be calculated, and for that sum to be paid to the personal representatives of the deceased partner. Alternatively, the partnership agreement can effectively prevent the death of a partner from amounting to any form of dissolution, by providing that the share of the partnership assets due to the representatives of a deceased partner be satisfied from the proceeds of an insurance policy covering the death of any partner. This approach to the death of a partner has the advantages of preserving the partnership assets intact, and provides for effective continuation of the family business irrespective of the identity of the partners of that business.

1 See Chapter 4.
2 Although the parties so entitled may be the remaining partners.

## RETIREMENT

**2.20** There is no right at common law for a partner unilaterally to retire from a partnership. The family partnership agreement should therefore contain an express power to permit a partner to retire from the partnership, if that is the intention of the partners.[1] The partnership should also consider whether the partnership agreement should permit more than one partner to retire at the same time. Thus the partnership agreement may provide that a partner cannot give notice of retirement while a previously served retirement notice served by a co-partner is still current.[2] The family partnership must generally seek to regulate the retirement of its partners, since this may have repercussions for the management of the partnership, for the balance of power within the partnership, and financial consequences if the partnership is to provide an annuity for the retiring partner.

1 See 30 *Forms & Precedents* Form 2, clause 21. This is an example of a standard clause permitting a partner to retire on giving prescribed notice to his co-partners. Such a clause should not prevent the other partner(s) from suspending or expelling the retiring partner prior to the expiry of the notice period. The clause may prescribe an age at which a partner must retire. This should be the same age for partners of both sexes.
2 See ibid Form 107.

**2.21** A partner may retire from an insolvent partnership. The partner may sell his partnership share to his co-partners. In the absence of fraud, the sale cannot be prevented under the insolvency legislation. A partner must not seek to remove partnership assets from the partnership business when retiring from an insolvent family partnership, as by doing so he may be held to be a party to a fraud on the partnership creditors.[1]

1 Insolvency Act 1986, ss 339, 340, 423.

## BANKRUPTCY

**2.22** It is particularly important for a family partnership that the bankruptcy of one of the partners does not result in the dissolution of the partnership. Section 33(1) of the Partnership Act 1890 provides that subject to the agreement of the partners, the bankruptcy of a partner dissolves the partnership. The partnership agreement should therefore provide that the bankruptcy of a partner may be grounds for expulsion of that person from the partnership, but that the partnership continues nevertheless.[1]

1 This will not prevent the separate creditors of the bankrupt partner seeking to make claims against that partner's partnership share in satisfaction of his debts. See Chapter 6.

## EXPULSION

**2.23** It is sensible for the partnership agreement to make provision for the expulsion of a partner for material breaches of any terms in the partnership agreement, or on the occurrence of certain prescribed events.[1] Such a power should enable a problem partner to be effectively removed from the partnership without preventing the continuation of the partnership by the other partners. This power of expulsion has been considered within the context of the protection of the minority partner, see Chapter 5, para 5.11. It is essential that the partnership agreement is precise as to what will constitute material breaches of partnership obligations, or what events will give rise to the right to expel. The power to expel will usually require that the partner to be expelled be served with notice setting out the grounds upon which expulsion is sought. The partnership agreement should specify the exact terms of any notice, and the number of partners required in order to exercise the power of expulsion. The partnership agreement should prescribe a procedure and the appropriate conduct of any hearings to be held as part of the expulsion process.

1 See 30 *Forms & Precedents* Form 1, para 18.

## CONSEQUENCES OF TERMINATION

**2.24** The consequences that flow from the technical dissolution of a partnership on the leaving, or expulsion, of a partner must be considered.[1] Where the partner leaves the partnership it may be sensible for the family partnership agreement to obtain an option to acquire that partner's share provided it is independently valued.

1 See ibid Form 1, para 19.


## DISSOLUTION AND WINDING-UP

**2.25** Consideration should be given to making provision in a family partnership agreement for a given partner or a prescribed number of partners to have the right to dissolve the partnership on giving the appropriate notice to the remaining partners.[1]

1 For a consideration of the nature of dissolution see Chapters 3 and 5. The power to dissolve a partnership on notice has been considered within the context of minority protection in Chapter 5. See 30 *Forms & Precedents* Form 1, para 20.


## PENSIONS

**2.26** The family partnership is intended to be a business which will exist for generations. The problem of the retirement of partners will arise frequently. The family partnership must address this issue. There are two approaches to this problem. The partnership may provide that on retirement a partner[1] will be entitled to an annuity from the partnership. However, a more modern approach is to place the financial burden on the partners individually, who will make provision for pensions out of their respective share of the profits of the business. The modern approach is preferable because of the tax advantages that it offers.[2]

1 And on the death of the former partner the right passes to his or her spouse.
2 See 30 *Forms & Precedents* Form 2, clause 19.

**2.27** Where however, annuities are to be paid to a retired partner or his dependants, which is not uncommon in relation to the founding partners of the family business, then the partnership agreement must specify whether provision is to be made for the spouse, children or for other dependants such as cohabitants who are also parents with the deceased partner.[1] The partnership agreement should provide that the annuities can be paid to the personal representatives of the deceased partner.[2] Inflation may be under control at the present time but it has been an otherwise constant factor in the business affairs of post war Britain. The partnership agreement should provide therefore for the annuity to be increased over a period of time.[3]

1 See 30 *Forms & Precedents* Forms 70 and 71.
2 See ibid Form 72.
3 Under a so-called escalation clause, see ibid Form 73.

## INSURANCE

**2.28** The family partnership, like all partnerships, is an unincorporated enterprise. All of its members will therefore be jointly and severally liable for the tortious activity of any member who commits such an act within the course of the partnership business.[1] Such liability would require adequate professional liability indemnity insurance within the context of a professional partnership.[2] This is in addition to the need for most family businesses to carry insurance in respect of the partnership assets, and to cover the loss of a partner's services through accident or illness.[3]

1 Partnership Act 1890, ss 10–12.
2 The carrying on of certain professions may require the relevant enterprise to carry such insurance, prime examples being solicitors and accountants.
3 See 30 *Forms & Precedents* Form 1, para 16.

## ILLNESS OR PREGNANCY OF PARTNERS

**2.29** A common occurrence in the family partnership will be the illness or pregnancy of a partner. Such events will put the average family partnership under considerable strain, with the remaining partners being left to carry out the duties of the absent partner. The partner who is absent from the partnership may need financial support. The partnership agreement should therefore specify the duration of such financial support and the circumstances in which it may be terminated. The agreement should also contain a power to expel a partner whose illness has made him or her permanently incapable of continuing as a partner.

**2.30** Many family partnership agreements should make provision for a female partner to enjoy maternity leave.[1] It should be noted that the provisions of the Sex Discrimination Act 1975[2] apply to partnerships, but a family partnership may nevertheless, lawfully discriminate against a woman, for example in the way the partnership affords her access to benefits. Thus a woman partner who has had maternity leave can lawfully receive slightly less pension provision than a male or female partner of equal standing in the partnership without the partnership facing an allegation of discrimination.

1 See 30 *Forms & Precedents* Form 2, clause 11, Form 87, clause 11, Form 88, clause 12. Precedent clause 12.2 provides for a male partner to enjoy paternity rights. The clause however, gives a much more restricted paternity right to a male partner than the equivalent maternity right to a female partner.
2 As amended by the Sex Discrimination Act 1986, s 1(3).

## ARBITRATION

**2.31** A partnership is a business relationship which is personal, a family partnership particularly so. Disputes between family partners can involve costly and time-consuming legal disputes which are damaging to long-term family relationships. It would therefore be advisable for the family partnership agreement to provide that disputes should be resolved by arbitration. Accordingly, the partnership agreement should contain an arbitration clause.[1] It is not sensible to appoint an official arbitrator, such as the President of the Law Society, who is most unlikely to have the time or the inclination to undertake arbitration in the event of this type of dispute. Where the family partnership is a professional practice, it is better to provide that if the partners cannot agree on the identity of the arbitrator, then the arbitrator should be appointed by an appropriate official of the governing body of the relevant profession.[2] It is suggested that the arbitration clause should cover disputes arising or continuing after the dissolution of the partnership.

1 See 30 *Forms & Precedents* Form 2, clause 27.
2 See ibid Form 88, clause 37.

## MEDIATION

**2.32** As an alternative to arbitration, the partners in a family partnership may seek to resolve their disputes by mediation or the involvement of independent experts.

## THE FAMILY COMPANY

**2.33** The family company as a private limited company is a entity distinct from its members. This is in direct contrast to the partnership. The family members will participate in the affairs of the company either in the guise of directors and/or shareholders.

## DIRECTORS

**2.34** The appointment of a family member to be a director of the company confers powers upon him, and creates a relationship between him and the company and the other family members as shareholders. The director of the company also owes responsibilities to the creditors of the company.[1] The major problem with regard to the family company is that classic company law doctrine divides the responsibilities of the management of the business between shareholders and directors, with the delegation of managerial powers to the directors. This division of responsibility was created with the model of the large public company as the business enterprise in mind. In these cases the directors would hold minority shareholdings and would be subject to the overall control of the majority shareholders, who could remove them if necessary in a meeting of the shareholders. In the case of the family company, the directors will usually have either a majority shareholding in the company, or at least be able to control voting power at the meetings of shareholders. In these cases the dual role of director/shareholder becomes crucial.

1 See Neill LJ in *Fulham Football Club Ltd v Cabra Estates plc* [1992] BCC 863 at 876, CA.

**2.35** The directors of a family company have the power to manage the company. They are the agents of the company and their authority stems from that position.[1] Directors are not however, the agents of the shareholders of the company.[2] In most family companies the directors are also the shareholders, although some of the family members will simply be shareholders in the company. However, if a director undertakes a transaction on behalf of a particular shareholder, then he may be an agent of that shareholder and will owe fiduciary duties to that individual.[3]

1 This should be compared with the position of the partners in a family company who are agents for each other (Partnership Act 1890, s 5).
2 *Gramophone and Typewriter Ltd v Stanley (Surveyor of Taxes)* [1908] 2 KB 89 at 105–106 per Buckley LJ, CA.
3 *Briess v Woolley* [1954] AC 333, [1954] 1 All ER 909, HL.


## ARTICLES OF ASSOCIATION

**2.36** Where reg 70 of Table A of the Companies Regulations 1985, SI 1985/805 applies to a company, then the management of the company is conferred on the directors. However, the power thus conferred is restricted to the exercise of the normal management powers of the business.[1] The articles of association may however, provide that although the general power of management of the business rests with the directors, certain specified matters may be subject to veto by one or more directors.[2] Members of a family company are strongly advised to take this approach to the management of the company.[3] Regulation 70, even when applicable to a company, is subject to the provisions of the Companies Act 1985 and the Insolvency Act 1986. This legislation provides that some powers cannot be exercised by the directors or any individual, but only by the shareholders acting in a general meeting.[4]

1 Contrast the position of the partnership and in particular s 24(5) of the Partnership Act 1890 and the powers of the majority of the partners to determine ordinary matters of partnership business.
2 *Salmon v Quin & Axtens Ltd* [1909] 1 Ch 311, CA; affd sub nom *Quin & Salmon* [1909] AC 442, HL.
3 The director or directors who may have such a power of veto may be the founders of the family business. Certain powers of veto may be given to directors who otherwise participate little in the affairs of the company, but who wish to have control over certain aspects of the affairs of the company and perhaps to protect their investment as shareholders.
4 It is beyond the scope of this book to list these principal powers. See Prime & Scanlan *The Law of the Private Limited Company*, Chapter 6. Examples include the power to alter the objects of the company (Companies Act 1985, s 4) the change of the company's name (s 28 ibid), to approve substantial property transactions with directors (s 320 ibid).


## REVERSION OF POWERS TO THE SHAREHOLDERS

**2.37** Deadlock between the directors in a family company is not uncommon. It would therefore be sensible for the articles of association to empower the shareholders to take back the powers of management vested in the directors.[1] The management of the family enterprise may therefore be entrusted to a limited number of the family members. This is broadly similar to the situation that may occur in the family partnership where s 24(5) of the Partnership Act 1890 is excluded by provision in the partnership agreement.[2]

1 See *Barron v Potter* [1914] 1 Ch 895; *Foster v Foster* [1916] 1 Ch 532. In the absence of such reversion, the shareholders have no power to supervise or otherwise control the exercise by the directors of the powers of management vested in them. *Howard Smith Ltd v Ampol Petroleum Ltd* [1974] AC 821 at 837 per Lord Wilberforce, PC.
2 For the nature of s 24(5) see para 2.2 above.

## MANAGING DIRECTOR

**2.38** Article 84 of Table A, if adopted by a company, permits the directors to appoint one of their number as managing director of the company, and to delegate some of their powers to him. The director thus appointed acts as the chief executive of the company. The managing director may therefore perform the functions normally exercised by the directors of the company acting as a board. The role is similar to that of a managing partner.[1]

1 See reg 72 of Table A.

## DUTIES OF THE DIRECTOR

**2.39** The directors of the family company owe duties to the company. The first duty so owed is a duty of care. The standard of competence that needs to be observed by, or expected from, a director in carrying out his duties is determined by reference to his individual knowledge and experience.[1] The director of the family company need not attend to the affairs of the company full-time. Where this is desired, the company should make provision to this effect in a contract made between the director and the company. However, in practice it may be that the family company with few employees will by necessity impose upon its directors the obligation to devote their efforts full-time to the affairs of the company.

1 *Re Brazilian Rubber Plantations and Estates Ltd* [1911] 1 Ch 425 at 427 per Neville J, *Re Elgindata Ltd* [1991] BCLC 959 at 994 per Warner J.

## FIDUCIARY DUTIES

**2.40** The directors of the family company owe fiduciary duties to the company. These duties can only be enforced by the company and not by the shareholders.[1] It therefore follows that the directors must exercise their powers 'bona fide in what they consider – not what a court may consider – is in the interests of the company, and not for any collateral purpose'.[2] The courts will not therefore interfere in the exercise of a director's powers, simply because the court would exercise the powers in what it considers is the best interests of the company. Where a director does exercise his powers improperly, the court may intervene. It may do so by granting an injunction to prevent the implementation of an improper exercise of power, and by ordering rescission where possible, of any contract made between the company and the director. If the directors act in good faith in the exercise of their powers, although for an improper purpose, then irrespective of their belief, they are in breach of their fiduciary duties.[3]

1 *Lee v Chou Wen Hsien* [1984] 1 WLR 1202, PC. Contrast the position in the case of the family partnership where the partners owe fiduciary duties inter se.
2 Per Lord Greene MR *Re Smith & Fawcett Ltd* [1942] Ch 304 at 306, CA.
3 *Hogg v Cramphorn Ltd* [1967] Ch 254, [1966] 3 All ER 420. Although such a breach could be the subject of ratification by the members of the company in general meeting.

**2.41** The duties noted above are owed to the company as an entity as distinct from the shareholders. Consequently, where the interests of the company are at variance with some of the company's members, then the directors will be justified in giving priority to the interests of the company.[1]

1 And indirectly the interests of the majority shareholders in most cases. See *Gaiman v National Association for Mental Health* [1971] Ch 317, [1970] 2 All ER 362.

## THE RULES AGAINST PROFITING

**2.42** The director of a family company must not put himself in a position where his interests conflict with that of the company. He must not therefore profit personally from any transactions in which the company may have a conflicting interest.[1] Furthermore, a director of the company may not enter into transactions with the company from which he will profit.[2] Nevertheless, if regs 85, 86 and 94 of Table A apply, a director of a company may undertake certain activities which would otherwise be prohibited under the principles noted above, provided that he has disclosed to the directors the nature and extent of his material interest, and he does not vote on the issue at any meeting of the directors which considers the matter. These provisions are based on the premise that if an interest is declared to the board by the director, the directors who do not share the interest will be sufficiently independent to ensure that the company's interests are safeguarded. In many family companies however, the directors or the majority of the directors may collectively share the interest, and disclosure to the board of that interest constitutes no safeguard of the company's interests.[3] In these circumstances the interests of the minority director/shareholder may be inadequately protected and the position may be compared with that of the minority partner in a family partnership.[4] It should be noted that the directors in their role as shareholders may approve a transaction undertaken by the directors in general meeting, unless the approval would constitute a fraud on the minority.[5]

1 *Regal (Hastings) Ltd v Gulliver* [1967] 2 AC 134n.
2 *Aberdeen Rly Co v Blaikie Bros* (1854) 1 Macq 461, HL.
3 Except where the ratification of the transaction constitutes a fraud on the minority, see Chapter 5.
4 Note also the Companies Act 1985, s 317 which imposes a duty on a director of a company who is in any way, whether directly or indirectly, interested in a contract or proposed contract with the company to declare the nature of his interest at a meeting of the directors of the company.
5 See Chapter 5.

## DUTIES TO INDIVIDUAL SHAREHOLDERS

**2.43** It is a general principle that the directors of a company owe no duty to individual shareholders, even in the case of a family company. The only remedy available to the shareholder where directors act contrary to the interests of the company, is to bring a derivative action.[1] However, in the case of *Allen v Hyatt*,[2] the directors approached the shareholders of the company requesting options to purchase the shares, and stating that this would help negotiations which they were undertaking on behalf of the company, which it was hoped would result in an amalgamation with another company. The options were given by the shareholders to the directors and they exercised the options making a significant profit. When the shareholders brought an action, the court held that the directors had constituted themselves as agents of the shareholders and had owed them fiduciary duties which they had breached.[3]

1 See Chapter 5. But see *Percival v Wright* [1902] 2 Ch 421, and para 2.46.
2 (1914) 30 TLR 444, PC.
3 The case was distinguished on this ground from that of *Percival v Wright* noted above.

**2.44** The imposition upon directors of a general fiduciary duty to the shareholders was not unambiguously accepted by the English courts until recently, not even in the case of the family company. However, commonwealth jurisdictions have shown a greater willingness to impose such liability. *Coleman v Myers*[1] concerned an old established company, whose shares had been held by the members of the Myers family for three generations. The chairman's son D took the position of managing director of the company. D enjoyed only a small shareholding in the company, and he made it clear to the other members of the family that he would only undertake the responsibilities of managing director if he was given a substantial holding in the company. With the assistance of his father he contracted to buy two large blocks of shares, agreeing to pay for these shares six months after acquisition. However, D intended to use his increased shareholding to engineer the sale of valuable property owned by the company, and to ensure that the company lent him the money to pay for the shares he had contracted to buy.

1 [1977] 2 NZLR 225.

**2.45** Some of the family members as shareholders objected to D's actions and mounted a campaign to prevent D from achieving his aims. D subsequently tried to take over the company. The price at which D offered to purchase the controlling shares was based on the report of an independent valuer who had not been informed that the company's property, and in particular its buildings, was highly undervalued in the company's books. The deals went through and D made a considerable profit as a consequence. A minority of the shareholders of the company brought an action on the grounds that their position had been prejudiced. They alleged inter alia that D as a director had breached his fiduciary duty towards them. The court held that both D and his father in their roles of managing director and chairman, owed fiduciary duties to the shareholders of the company. A particularly crucial factor in the court making this determination, was that the company was a family company. Furthermore, because of the nature of the company, the directors had an intimate knowledge of the company and its affairs. The circumstances both of the company and the relationship of its members created a relationship of confidence which was imposed upon the directors in the giving of financial and commercial advice. D breached the fiduciary duties owed to the shareholders in his conduct and by his dealings.[1]

1 The court refused to follow *Percival v Wright*.


ENGLISH AUTHORITY

**2.46** The case of *Myers* has recently been followed in England. In *Re Chez Nico (Restaurants) Ltd*,[1] Browne-Wilkinson VC refused to accept the proposition in *Percival v Wright* that directors could deal in shares in their company without revealing the knowledge they gained as directors in the company. *The* *court approved both the decision and reasoning of the case of Myers.* The court was of the opinion that in certain circumstances fiduciary duties, which imposed a duty of disclosure, could arise between the directors of a company and its shareholders.[2]

1 [1992] BCLC 192.
2 At 208. Such an inference is more likely to be made in the case of a family company.

**2.47** Despite the above authorities, it remains difficult to assert that the directors of a family company owe a general fiduciary duty to its shareholders. The above authorities, although involving companies which may be regarded as family companies, are concerned with specific circumstances and it is difficult to see how they could apply to situations outside their own specific facts. The continuing absence of any generally applicable fiduciary duty owed by directors to shareholders even in a family company, is perhaps the greatest contrast between the company and the partnership, where the partners who control the activities of the business nevertheless owe fiduciary duties to their fellow partners.

DUTIES BETWEEN SHAREHOLDERS

**2.48** The actions of the directors in conducting the business of the company may involve a breach of duty to the company. The shareholders may however ratify such actions in a meeting.[1] Where the directors are also the majority shareholders, the ratification may amount to little more than a fiction. The question therefore arises as to whether the members of the company owe a duty to the company, and more particularly to their fellow members, when exercising their votes. It seems clear from the case of *Pender v Lushington*[2] that a shareholder may vote entirely in his own interests in a meeting of shareholders, although his actions may be entirely contrary to the interests of the company as a whole and to his fellow shareholders.[3] It has also been held that a shareholder, even a director/shareholder, may vote in his own interest at a meeting of the shareholders with respect to a contract made between the company and himself.[4]

1 However, where such ratification constitutes a fraud on the minority shareholders the latter may seek, through a derivative action, to contest the validity of that ratification. See Chapter 5.
2 (1877) 6 Ch D 70.
3 This is subject to statutory modification, see for example the Companies Act 1985, s 164(2) and (5).
4 *North-West Transportation Co and Beatty v Beatty* (1887) 12 App Cas 589, PC.

CIRCUMSTANCES IN WHICH SHAREHOLDERS MUST VOTE IN THE BEST INTERESTS OF THE COMPANY

**2.49** The position remains unclear, but it has been held by the courts that, despite the above, majority shareholders must, in certain restricted circumstances, exercise their voting powers bona fide and in the best interests of the company.[1] These circumstances, which are noted in note 1 above, are however restricted and do not effect the general position of shareholders stated in *Pender v Lushington*. This contrasts with the position of the members of a partnership who cannot, in exercising their votes at a partnership meeting, ignore the interests of the partnership or the other members, if by doing so they are in breach of their fiduciary duties to the partnership and the other partners.

1 *Allen v Gold Reefs of West Africa Ltd* [1900] 1 Ch 656, CA. Thus the majority shareholders must so vote when:
   (a) altering the articles of association of the company;
   (b) on the appointment of a director;
   (c) at a meeting of class members;
   (d) the members are voting on whether the company should take legal action to enforce its rights against persons who effectively control the company, when the latter have acted illegally or ultra vires as regards the company's powers or fraudulently. See also *Harris v A Harris Ltd* 1936 SC 183.

DIRECTORS – FINANCIAL PROVISION

**2.50** There is no right for directors to be remunerated for their services unless the articles of association so provide. Where reg 82 of Table A of the Companies Act 1985 has been adopted by a family company, the directors shall be remunerated as may be determined by ordinary resolution. It would, however, be advisable for the company and the directors to regulate their relationship by a contract of employment. Pension provision on the retirement of the director may prove expensive for the family company. The family company may, as in the case of a partnership, leave pension provision to the directors. Where the company makes provision for pensions for its directors, it must[1] show the aggregate amount of directors' or past directors' pensions in a note to its accounts.[2] There is an elaborate set of statutory provisions in the Companies Act 1985 which require a company to set out in its accounts payments to directors in respect of their services or sums paid in respect of compensation for loss of office.[3] These provisions, although designed to protect the company from directors awarding themselves substantial and unmerited rewards, have little meaning within the context of the family company.[4]

1 Unless it is a small company see Sch 8, para 12 inserted by SI 1992/2452.
2 Schedule 6, para 7(1).
3 For example see s 312 and s 313(1) which also require the approval of the company.
4 Especially since the disclosure provisions do not apply to bona fide payments by way of damages for breach of contract or by way of pension in respect of past services ibid s 316(3)).

TERMINATION OF OFFICE

**2.51** The Companies Act 1985 does not provide any mechanism for the vacation of the office of director. However, it would be sensible for the company to make such provision. If reg 81 of Table A has been adopted by the company then the office of director will be vacated in the following circumstances:

(a) He ceases to be director by virtue of any provision in the Companies Act, or he is otherwise prohibited from holding the office of director;
(b) He becomes bankrupt or makes a composition or arrangement with his creditors;
(c) He has been admitted to hospital because he is suffering from a mental disorder or is subject to the jurisdiction of the court of protection in matters concerning mental disorder;

(d) He resigns his office by giving notice to the company; or
(e) He has been absent from meetings of the directors for a consecutive period of six months without the permission of the directors, and the directors resolve that his office be vacated.

These provisions are comparable to the provisions for the removal of a partner from a family partnership noted in para 2.23. It would be advisable for a family company to adopt such provisions in its articles of association.

RETIREMENT

**2.52** It is perfectly possible for the family company to make no provision for the retirement of a director. The regulations may, however, provide for retirement of the directors by rotation.[1] If the company has adopted Table A then unless this is the intention of the company, the articles will have to be amended. It should be noted that if Table A has been adopted by a family company, then a managing director and any other director holding an executive office within the company are not subject to the retirement rotation provisions.[2] If the articles of the company provide for the retirement of the director on reaching retirement age, then the articles may further provide for the director to resubmit himself for re-election by vote of the members on special resolution.

1 Regulations 73 and 74.
2 Regulation 84.

REMOVAL

**2.53** Section 303 of the Companies Act 1985 provides that a director may be removed from office. Notwithstanding any provision in the articles, a director may be removed under this statutory provision by ordinary resolution.[1] The removal of the director under this provision does not prevent the company being in breach of any contract that the director may have with the company. Compensation payable to a director in these circumstances may be expensive, but may be worth paying if the director is seriously damaging the interests of the company. However, the family company is particularly vulnerable to the possibility of the entrenched director, by virtue of what may be called a *Bushell v Faith* provision.

1 For the nature of an ordinary resolution see Chapter 5, para 5.28, n 2.

**2.54** In the case of *Bushell v Faith*,[1] a private limited company was incorporated by the plaintiff and her mother.[2] At the time of the action 100 shares were held by the plaintiff and 100 shares by the plaintiff's brother, who was the defendant in the action. In addition 100 shares were held by the plaintiff's sister. Both the plaintiff and her brother were directors of the company. The plaintiff sought to have the defendant removed from his office of director, and sought the aid of her sister.

1 [1970] AC 1099, [1990] 1 All ER 53, HL.
2 It could therefore be regarded as a family company.

**2.55** At a general meeting the resolution proposed the removal of the defendant. The resolution was approved by 2 to 1 on a show of hands. The defendant demanded a vote by poll. He then claimed he was entitled to cast 300 votes against the resolution and the resolution was defeated. The basis of the defendant's claim was a provision in the company's articles which provided that:

> 'In the event of a resolution being proposed at any general meeting of the company for the removal from office of any director any shares held by that director shall on a poll in respect of such a resolution carry the right to three votes per share.'

**2.56** The plaintiff maintained that the article was invalid as being contrary to s 184 of the Companies Act 1948.[1] At first instance Ungoed-Thomas J agreed with the plaintiff's contention that giving effect to the article would render otiose the statutory power to remove a director by ordinary resolution. The appellate courts disagreed with this view. The House of Lords by a majority of 4 to 1 upheld the article. The House of Lords held that what is now s 303 merely prevented the articles of association of a company from prescribing that a director can only be removed from office by a special or extraordinary resolution.[2] However, the court also held that since the Companies Acts have never prohibited or prevented the granting of weighted voting rights on certain resolutions, then the validity of the relevant article could not be contested.

1 Now s 303 of the Companies Act 1985.
2 For the nature of these resolutions see Chapter 5, para 5.28, n 2.

**2.57** The case therefore recognises that the articles of association of a family company may provide for the entrenchment of the position of one or more of its directors by the mechanism of weighted voting.

PRE-EMPTION RIGHTS

**2.58** The family partnership can ensure that the membership of the business is restricted to immediate family members by provision in the partnership agreement. The Partnership Act 1890[1] provides that in the absence of contrary agreement, the admission of a new partner is a matter for unanimity. In the case of a company, it may be more difficult to achieve this aim in a family company. A family company as a private limited company is prohibited from offering its shares directly or indirectly to the public.[2] In the absence of pre-emption rights, a shareholder in a family company cannot prevent other family shareholders from selling their shares by private treaty to outsiders, or to other family members.[3] Pre-emption rights may be defined as a right given to shareholders to buy the shares of any other shareholder of the company who wishes to sell his shareholding.[4]

1 Section 24(5). See para 2.2 above.
2 Companies Act 1985, s 81.
3 With the common and undesired consequence that the balance of power in the company is upset.
4 The term may also refer to the right of a shareholder to subscribe for further shares on a new issue made by the company so as to preserve as far as possible, the relative proportion of shares held in the company. See also ss 89 and 90 of the Companies Act 1985 which governs such rights. A family company may provide in its articles of association, or even in its memorandum of association, that shares may be issued without offering them to existing members, see ss 80, 81 and 95(1) and (2) of the Companies Act 1985.

**2.59** Many family companies provide in their articles of association that a shareholder wishing to dispose of his shares is obliged to offer those shares to other members of the company before disposing of them to outsiders.[1] This right only amounts to a right of first refusal, and a member of the company who cannot take advantage of the right may find that the shares may then be acquired by a rival present member of the company or an outsider, permanently disturbing the balance of power in the company to his detriment. However, where the directors of the company seek to issue shares primarily in order to alter the balance of power in the company, they may be prevented from doing so by a member of the company.[2]

1 Until the Companies Act 1980, a private limited company had to restrict the right to transfer its shares, see the Companies Act 1948, s 28. Private limited companies usually provided in their articles that no shares could be transferred to a non-member if a member could be found to purchase the shares at a fair price. Many older companies still have this form of provision in their articles. Furthermore, many companies incorporated since the passing of the Companies Act 1980 still incorporate such a provision in their articles, although they are no longer obliged to do so. The usual provision in such cases takes the form of a pre-emption right, a right of first refusal being given to a member of the company when another member seeks to dispose of his shares in the company.
2 See *Clemens v Clemens Bros Ltd* [1976] 2 All ER 268 discussed in Chapter 5, para 5.35.

**2.60** Many older family companies may provide in their articles of association[1] that the directors may refuse to register any share transfers. Such a provision gives the directors, at their absolute discretion, the power to refuse to register any transfer of shares without any obligation to give reasons for doing so.[2] Any provision of this kind is the most effective means of ensuring that the shares of a company continue to be held by members of the family. The courts have held that the directors must exercise their power of refusal to register in good faith, and with regard to the interests of the company as a whole and not their own interests as directors/shareholders.[3]

1 In order that they qualified as private companies within the terms of the Companies Act 1948, s 28 see para 2.59 and n 1 above.
2 In order for the provision to be entirely effective, it should require the consent of the directors to transfer the beneficial ownership in any company shares. This would prevent the transferor holding the shares on trust for the benefit of the transferee.
3 *Re Smith & Fawcett Ltd* [1942] Ch 304, [1942] 1 All ER 542, CA; *Re Swaledale Cleaners Ltd* [1968] 3 All ER 619, [1968] 1 WLR 1710, CA.

**2.61** If the courts are satisfied that any refusal to register a transfer of shares has been exercised in bad faith, then the party seeking to have the transfer registered may seek the following remedies:

(a) An order for rectification of the register under s 359 of the Companies Act 1985;
(b) Relief under s 459–461 of the Companies Act 1985;[1]
(c) An order for winding up the company under s 122(1)(g) of the Insolvency Act 1986.[2]

1 See Chapter 5.
2 See Chapter 5. This remedy is draconian and the courts may be reluctant to grant the remedy in cases where the party has been the subject of a refusal to register a share transfer. The courts in such instances, may grant an injunction to the directors to restrain the party from seeking the winding up of the company, *Charles Forte Investments Ltd v Amanda* [1964] Ch 240, [1963] 2 All ER 940, CA.

## AUTHORITY OF DIRECTORS

**2.62** The directors of the company as its agents may bind the company in any transactions under the normal principles of agency.[1] If a director exceeds his authority and binds the company, the company may take legal action against the director unless the company ratifies the director's action.[2]

[1] These issues have been considered above para 2.3 within the context of the partnership.
[2] This may give rise to problems where the minority shareholder(s) do not wish that the actions of a director be ratified see Chapter 5.


## CONCLUSION – SHAREHOLDER AGREEMENTS

**2.63** The controls that shareholders have over a family company are restricted for the reasons set out above. In the case of minority shareholders, their power to influence company policy may be severely circumscribed. The requirement that certain matters require the approval of the shareholders acting in general meeting by prescribed majorities[1] vests little influence in those shareholders, since in most family companies the directors/shareholders will generally control sufficient voting power to secure the passing of any resolution. The family company is a less flexible vehicle for giving effect to the interests of the individual members of the business than the partnership. The family members of a business may nevertheless seek the various advantages that incorporation of the business offers,[2] but also seek to ensure that the interests of all the family members are addressed and recognised within the effective operation of the business. The company's constitutional documents are not sufficiently flexible in this regard. Company lawyers have therefore resorted to the use of the shareholder agreement. The shareholder agreement may be used so to effect a partnership-type agreement between the members of the company within the framework of the limited liability company.

[1] See Chapter 5 where special and extraordinary resolutions are considered.
[2] See Chapter 1.


## CONTENTS OF SHAREHOLDER AGREEMENTS

**2.64** An examination of a typical shareholder agreement will show certain similarities to a partnership agreement.[1] The effect of the shareholder agreement is to create a business vehicle not unlike a limited partnership,[2] but in which the members can participate in the business without losing the benefit of limited liability.[3] The shareholder agreement will be valid as a contract between the shareholders. It will also bind the company and the shareholders provided that the agreement does not require the company to undertake a responsibility or commitment which it is unable in law to promise.[4] To the extent that the company does make such undertakings, the courts may be prepared to sever those parts of the agreement and enforce the parts of the shareholder agreement which regulate the relationship between the shareholders inter se.

[1] See Vol 19 *Forms & Precedents* and the appendix to Prime & Scanlan *The Law of Private Limited Companies*.
[2] See Chapter 14 Prime & Scanlan *The Law of Partnership* for a consideration of this form of partnership.

3 Although the shareholder agreement is usually created and entered into by the members of a company, so as to provide a firm and coherent business structure which is demanded by financial institutions before they will be prepared to lend money to the enterprise.
4 *Russell v Northern Bank Development Corpn Ltd* [1992] 3 All ER 161, [1992] 1 WLR 588, HL.

**2.65** The standard provisions contained in a shareholder agreement will be likely to include:[1]

(a) a term that the parties warrant the truth of the facts set out in any recitals;
(b) terms as to how the company is to be financed, and the responsibilities of the parties in relation thereto;
(c) terms governing the giving of guarantees and indemnities to third parties;
(d) terms as to the carrying on of the business of the company and the responsibilities of the parties and the company in relation thereto;

The above terms are central to the operation of a shareholder agreement in a family company. Such terms may determine the parties who will undertake the business of the company, usually the director/shareholders, and also impose particular duties upon those individuals. Thus the shareholder agreement may require the company to provide to its members on a regular basis copies of the company's accounts including the company's unaudited management accounts.[2]

(e) terms to restrict the manner in which the business of the company is to be carried on so as to protect the shareholders;

Such terms are essential to the protection of minority shareholders, and may, for example, restrict the power of the director/shareholders to effect changes in the articles of association or the memorandum of association, or to incur expenditure above a prescribed amount, or to enter into or vary any contract or arrangement with any of its directors or shareholders.

(f) terms restricting the freedom of the parties to deal with their shares including a share pre-emption clause or terms covering the shares of parties on cessation of their employment with the company.

The shareholder agreement may deal with procedures for dealing with a deadlock situation between the members of the company, where no one party or group of members can command a majority on an issue of company policy. The shareholder agreement may also contain clauses dealing with the illness of any director/shareholder of the company, or any matters which could be contained in a partnership agreement and which have been considered above in the context of the management of a family partnership.

Finally, the agreement should provide that it is a condition of the agreement that the parties cannot assign their rights under the agreement without the written consent of the other parties, and that it is a condition that any party acquiring shares in the company must become a party to the agreement. The agreement should not however make the parties partners, and should make express provision to this effect.

1 The list is not intended to be comprehensive.
2 These duties may be modelled on the duties that the members of a partnership owe one another inter se.

## CONCLUSIONS

**2.66** It is apparent from the above that the partnership as a business enterprise differs in several material respects from the private limited company. However, the use of the shareholder agreement has brought the operation of the family company very much closer to the operation of the family partnership. This development must be seen in conjunction with parallel developments in other aspects of the law governing business organisations, which is reducing the differences between the family company and the family partnership.[1]

1 See Chapters 5 and 6.

# Chapter 3

# Divorce and the family business

**3.1** The family business in either its incorporated or unincorporated form constitutes family property either directly or indirectly. Where the participants in the enterprise, or at least some of the participants, are married marital breakdown may not only cause emotional distress between the relevant parties but may have financial consequences, both for the parties and for the business.

THE BUSINESS AS FAMILY PROPERTY

**3.2** Where the family business is a private limited company, then the relevant family members will hold shares in the enterprise. Collectively the shares will give the participants the right to wind-up the company and to receive the assets of the company on its dissolution. However, until that event, the company enjoys full ownership in its assets. Accordingly, the family members will enjoy their shares in the family company as part of their personal estate.

**3.3** In the case of a family partnership, the relevant family members will enjoy a direct interest in the enterprise and the assets of that enterprise in proportion to their respective share in the partnership. The nominal separation of the partnership estate from that of the respective separate estates of the partners does not detract from the essential fact that an individual partner's estate is an amalgam of both his personal estate and his share in the family partnership.

**3.4** This chapter will consider in outline the consequences, both for the individual members of the family business and for the business itself, of one or more of the members being a party to a divorce. An outline will be given of the orders that a divorce court may make that would affect the proprietary rights of a member of a family business and the business itself, irrespective of whether the business is a company or a partnership.

THE DIVORCE SETTLEMENT AND THE FAMILY BUSINESS

**3.5** Under the Matrimonial Causes Act 1973,[1] a court hearing a petition for divorce, nullity or judicial separation has, by virtue of s 21 of the Act, the power to make one or more of the following orders against either spouse:[2]

(a) Unsecured periodical payments to the other spouse.
(b) Secured periodical payments to the other spouse.
(c) Lump sum payments to the other spouse.
(d) Unsecured periodical payments for any child of the family.
(e) Secured periodical payments for any child of the family; and/or
(f) A lump sum payment for any child of the family.

(The above orders are collectively known as financial provision orders.)

(g) Transfer of property to the other spouse or for the benefit of any child of the family.
(h) Settlement of property for the benefit of the other spouse or any child of the family.
(i) Variation of any ante-nuptial or post-nuptial settlement.

(The above orders are collectively known as property adjustment orders.)

Where a court makes a secured periodical payments order, a lump sum order or a property transfer order, it can in addition, order the sale of property belonging to either or both spouses.

1 Section s 21 as amended.
2 Accordingly such orders are not necessarily made in favour of the petitioner. Although the divorce or other matrimonial proceedings may involve a spouse who is not a member of the family business, the text will assume that both parties to the proceedings are members of the business unless the contrary is expressed.

**3.6** Although there are guidelines prescribed in the Act[1] which set out the matters which the court should take into account when exercising the powers to make any of the above orders,[2] it should be emphasised that considerable discretion is given to the judge in determining what order or orders will be made in any particular case.[3] The orders will now be considered in turn.

1 Matrimonial Causes Act 1973, s 25, as amended.
2 Further consideration is beyond the scope of this book. For a full review of these matters see *Bromley's Family Law* (8th edn, Butterworths, Chapter 21).
3 It should be noted that English law does not recognise any concept of community property, which would severely restrict a court from being able to redistribute property to the parties to a divorce.

PERIODICAL PAYMENTS

**Unsecured payments**

**3.7** Where the matrimonial proceedings result in the court making an order that one spouse make an unsecured payment to the other, the duration of the order is of importance. Such payments are intended for the maintenance of that spouse, and must terminate on that party's death. It will be usual, therefore, for the payments to come out of the paying spouse's income, and to end on that party's death.[1] Since the payments are from the payer's income, it is unlikely that such payments will adversely affect his estate or the financial health of any family business, or result in the winding up of the enterprise.

1 The payee could however, apply for an order under the Inheritance (Provision for Family and Dependants) Act 1975.

## Secured payments

**3.8** Secured payments are more attractive to the payee, since there is no problem in enforcing such payments. The payments are secured on the capital of the payer. By tying up the payer's capital in this way, the position of the payee will be protected even if the payer becomes bankrupt. Since the payments are secured, the payee can continue to benefit even after the death of the payer. It is usual for the payments to be smaller than an equivalent order for unsecured payments.[1]

1 Because of the supposed greater benefits of the secured order. See *Chichester v Chichester* [1936] P 129, [1936] 1 All ER 271.

**3.9** Payments are normally secured by the court ordering the paying spouse to transfer specific assets into a trust. The trustees will hold the property on trust to pay the sum ordered by the court to the payee, and any balance to the payer. Alternatively, the trustees may pay the income from the secured property to the paying spouse, but only if he complies with the court order, and will use the income, and if required, the capital if that party defaults. The court may, however, order specific property to be charged with the payment of the sum ordered. On termination of the court order, the capital must be returned to the payer or to that party's estate.

**3.10** Similar considerations to those noted above apply to unsecured and secured payments made in favour of the children of the family of a member or members of a family business.

## TAX IMPLICATIONS

**3.11** The Finance Act 1988 brought significant changes in the manner in which maintenance payments are dealt with for taxation purposes. Under the tax regime prior to the Finance Act 1988, the payer was able to deduct maintenance payments from his or her taxable income, and these were paid net after deduction of net tax. From 1988/89 however, payments are paid gross where the obligation to make payments arose after the enactment of the relevant provisions of the Finance Act 1988.[1] Accordingly, tax in these circumstances is not deducted at source and the payments do not form part of the taxable income of the payee. If the payment constitutes a qualifying payment,[2] a limited degree of tax relief is available to the payer, being the lesser of:

(a)  the amount of maintenance actually paid; and
(b)  an amount equal to the married couple's allowance for the tax year.

1 Generally on or after 15 March 1988.
2 A qualifying payment is a maintenance or periodical payment made under court order, or a written agreement under the aegis of the Child Support Act 1991, which is to take effect within the area of the EU or European Economic Area, and has been made; by one party to a marriage or former marriage either:
   (a) to or for the benefit of and for the maintenance of the other spouse; or
   (b) to the other spouse for the maintenance of a child of the family.

**3.12** Secured payments may also give rise to issues of both income and capital gains, depending on whether the payee is a spouse, former spouse or child of the family of the payer. Where the security has been created by way of a trust arrangement, and the payer has retained an interest in the settlement,[1] the payer, under normal circumstances, would be taxable on all trust income. There is however, an exemption for any such charge by virtue of s 660A of the Income and Corporation Taxes Act 1988, but only where the income arises under a settlement made solely to provide for a divorced or separated spouse.

1 The payer will generally be entitled to receive any excess income after satisfaction of the maintenance payments, and to have the secured property returned on the cessation of the obligation to make maintenance payments. See para 3.9 above.

**3.13** Although qualifying maintenance payments are tax-free in the hands of the payee, where the payee is a spouse or former spouse, any such payment received from a trust will be taxable income in the hands of the recipient, even where the trust was created after the qualifying date.[1] The situation with regard to secured payments to a child of the family is different. Although a secured maintenance agreement made on or after 15 March 1988 may be a settlement, by virtue of s 660B of the Incomes and Corporation Taxes Act 1988, income from the trust will be taxable as the payer's income and not that of the child. Furthermore, the transfer of the assets will constitute a deemed disposal of assets by the settlor, giving rise to possible capital gains liability. This tax liability can be minimised or avoided by recourse to certain stratagems. Thus assets could be transferred with a value which does not exceed the acquisition value[2] by more than the amount of the indexation allowance.[3] Transfers of assets could be made which are not chargeable to capital gains tax.[4]

1 15 March 1988, see para 3.11 n 1.
2 From which the liability to capital gains tax will be calculated.
3 The indexation allowance is an annual sum which can be transferred without attracting liability to capital gains tax.
4 For example transfers of sterling cash, if such sums are available to the settlor.

LUMP SUM PAYMENTS

**3.14** On the divorce, nullity or separation of a member or joint members of a family business, the court may order either party to pay a lump sum to the other. On rare occasions, such payments may be ordered in respect of a child of the family. The principal purpose of such payments is to adjust the parties' capital assets.

## Raising the funds

**3.15** The raising of the sums required to satisfy a lump sum payment may cause several legal and practical problems for the payer and for the family business of which he is a member. How such sums can be raised without too much financial disruption to the individual and the business, will first be considered in the context of the family company.

**3.16** If the money needed to make the lump sum payment can be raised from the family company without seriously damaging the enterprise, the principal concern will be to achieve this aim in the most tax-efficient way. The payer in a family company may have lent money to the company, the company in repaying the loan for the purposes of providing the required finance, will not give rise to any appreciable tax problems. Even if withdrawal of the loan for the above purposes may cause problems for the company, the payer may nevertheless withdraw the loan to provide the required finance for payment of the lump sum, and then take out a personal loan which he then transfers to the company. The interest on the personal loan would then be eligible for loan interest relief in the following circumstances:

(a) if the loan is to purchase ordinary shares or to make a loan to a close company;[1]
(b) the borrower is an individual who either;
   (i) alone or with certain associates has a material interest[2] in the company; or
   (ii) holds any ordinary shares and works for the greater part of his or her time in the management or conduct of the company or an associated company.[3]

1 Most family companies will be close companies. A close company is defined as a company registered in the United Kingdom, and which is controlled by five or less participants, or any number of participants who are directors of the company. That is provided that over half of the net assets of the company could be distributed to those directors, or to five or less participants on the notional winding-up of the company. See s 414 of the Income and Corporation Taxes Act 1988 as amended by s 104 of the Finance Act 1989.
2 Usually this requirement is satisfied by holding 5% or more of the company's ordinary share capital.
3 The situation noted above could be adopted in the case of a payer who was a member of a family partnership with similar tax advantages. The conditions for tax relief in such circumstances are:
   (a) the loan must be for the purchase of a share in or making an advance to a partnership;
   (b) the individual must be a member of the partnership, but not a limited partner within the terms of the Limited Partnership Act 1907; and
   (c) where the advance is to the partnership the money must be used for the purposes of the trade, profession or vocation.

**3.17** The family company may be able to borrow the money required to finance the lump sum payment.[1] The interest on the loan may be deductible, whereas interest on money borrowed by a payer to pay a spouse or former spouse a lump sum is not deductible for tax purposes.

1 The family company may be able to authorise such a payment without objection from shareholders, see Chapters 2 and 5.

**3.18** Despite the above, there may be restrictions on the powers of a family company to lend money to a director/shareholder.[1] It may therefore be a viable strategy for the director/shareholder to borrow the money required to finance the lump sum payment from an independent party, and then to secure an increase in the income received from the company in order to service the loan. This may be done either by increasing the payer's director's remuneration or by payment of an increased dividend on the shares that the payer holds in the company. Both of these approaches have difficulties which are considered below.

1 These restrictions may not exist in relation to a family partnership.

## DIRECTOR'S REMUNERATION

**3.19** The first problem for the company in increasing the remuneration of a director for the purposes noted above, is not only an increased tax liability for the director concerned, but also a potential increase in National Insurance contributions for the company. Furthermore, even in the case of a family company, it may prove impossible to increase the remuneration of one director without a pro rata increase in the remuneration of the other directors. Such an action may prove prohibitively expensive for the company.

## DIVIDENDS

**3.20** Similar considerations to those noted above would also apply to a proposed increase in dividends payable to a director/shareholder in order to service a loan for the purposes of making a lump sum payment to a spouse or former spouse. This remains the case despite the fact that it may be fiscally more efficient to receive income as dividends rather than as director's remuneration.

## PARTNERSHIPS

**3.21** In the case of a family partnership, any increase of drawings by a partner for the purpose of enabling that partner to meet his obligations under a financial provision order, may also give rise to problems. Irrespective of the terms of the partnership agreement which may permit such an action, the views of the other partners and their interests may conflict with that of the divorced partner. However, there are no problems with such a transaction of increased National Insurance contributions for the family business.

## PURCHASE BY A COMPANY OF ITS OWN SHARES

**3.22** The family company as a form of private limited company, may be in a position to buy back its own shares from the shareholder who is seeking to meet his obligations under a financial provision order. The advantage of this procedure is that the money is directed to the shareholder who requires it, without the need to make provision for the other shareholders in the business. The other shareholders are not normally adversely affected by such a transaction because the proportions of capital of the company represented by their shareholdings are proportionally increased. Nevertheless, the balance of voting power in the company may be affected by such a transaction. Where the other party to the divorce proceedings is also a shareholder in the family company, and is perceived with hostility by the other members of the company, or at least a faction of the members, then the purchase of the shares[1] of the spouse or former spouse of that party by the company may seriously upset the balance of power in the company. It may therefore be desirable in the above circumstances, to ensure that it is a condition of the acquisition of the shares of the party who is obliged to satisfy a financial provision order in favour of their spouse or former spouse and co-shareholder, that the recipient spouse is obliged to surrender all or a proportion of their holding in the company. Any proposed acquisition of shares by a family company in the above circumstances will be a more attractive proposition, where the relevant shareholder is a majority shareholder, and the acquisition is partial and will not result in that party losing control of the company.

1 Or even a proportion of those shares.

**3.23** The power of a family company to acquire its own shares is governed principally by s 162 of the Companies Act 1985. The main requirements are:

(a) that the company's articles of association permit such an acquisition;
(b) the purchase of the shares must be made out of distributable profits; and
(c) the purchase must be authorised by a special resolution of the company.

**3.24** It should be noted that, by virtue of s 171 of the Companies Act 1985, a private limited company may use capital to purchase its own shares. The amount of capital that may be used for this purpose is called the 'permissible capital payment'.[1] This is such an amount, as taken together with any available profits of the company and the proceeds of any fresh issue of shares made for the purposes of the redemption or purchase, which is equal to the price of the redemption or purchase.[2] Thus capital may only be used to the extent that the normal permissible sources of finance for these purposes are not available.

1 Companies Act 1985, ss 171(1) and (2).
2 Ibid s 171(3).

## FISCAL CONSEQUENCES OF ACQUISITION

**3.25** The power of a private limited company to acquire its own shares[1] may nevertheless give rise to issues of taxation. Without tax relief, the excess of the price paid for the shares over the capital originally subscribed, would constitute a distribution. The consequence of the transaction being regarded as a distribution is that it is effectively treated as a dividend. This results in the company having to pay advance corporation tax[2] and the shareholder suffering higher rate tax up to his marginal income tax rate.

1 This power was introduced by the Companies Act 1981.
2 For the nature of advance corporation tax see *Tiley & Collison's UK Tax Guide 1997–1998* Butterworths, Chapter 23. Note that the Chancellor in his November statement announced the proposed abolition of advance corporation tax from April 1999.

**3.26** The Finance Act 1982[1] provides, however, that subject to certain conditions, a payment by a company in respect of its own shares will only attract a capital gains tax liability in the hands of the vendor shareholder. The major conditions are:

(a) the company must be an unquoted company;
(b) the company must be a trading company or the holding company of such a company;
(c) the purchase of the shares must be wholly or mainly for the benefit of company's trade;[2]
(d) it must not be a transaction carried out with a tax-avoidance motive;
(e) the vendor shareholder must satisfy residence and a minimum period of ownership requirements; and
(f) as a result of the transaction the vendor's shareholding must be eliminated or substantially redeemed. Thus the proportion of the company's issued share capital held by the shareholder after the transaction must not exceed 75% of that held immediately before the transaction.

1 Finance Act 1982, Part III.
2 There is no reason why the purchase of the shares for the purposes of permitting the relevant shareholder to satisfy his obligations to his spouse or former spouse should not come within the terms of this requirement.

**3.27** If all of the above requirements are met, then the proceeds of the sale in the hands of the vendor will be treated as income rather than capital gains. With the present tax regime, this may constitute a small benefit to the vendor shareholder.

PARTNERSHIPS

**3.28** There is no equivalent procedure to that noted above when the family business is conducted as a partnership. Since the partnership is not an entity which is distinct from its constituent members, there is no business enterprise independent from the members which can purchase a partner's partnership share. The other partners or one other partner can,[1] however, purchase a part or the entirety of a partner's share in order to provide the capital for that partner to fulfil his obligation under a financial provision order. The proceeds of the sale in the hands of that partner will be chargeable to capital gains tax. The issue of the balance of power within the partnership will arise in such cases. These issues have been considered above in connection with the acquisition by a company of its own shares see para 3.22.

1 If the partnership agreement permits, or the partners consent to the transaction.

**3.29** Funds could be made available for a family company to purchase shares from one of its shareholders by recourse to the company's pension fund. It must be emphasised that this may, however, be regarded as a risky venture. If the company fails, its employees may be left without employment and with reduced pensions. In the case of a family company, the employees may be family members. Furthermore, by virtue of the Pensions Act 1995, a pension fund cannot invest more than 5% of its assets in the employer. Accordingly, unless the sum required to purchase the shares is small, it is unlikely that the company pension fund could make a significant contribution.

SALE OF SHARES TO A THIRD PARTY

**3.30** The sale of shares in the company to a third party in order to raise the funds to satisfy a financial provision order, is the least likely option available to the shareholder in a family company. The principal difficulty for the shareholder in these circumstances, is to find a third party willing to purchase what is frequently a minority interest in the company. Apart from the problem of valuing such shares, the vendor shareholder may find that without the consent of the directors/shareholders, the registration of the potential purchaser as a member[1] of the company may be refused. The position of a purchaser in the above circumstances is that unless the relevant transaction is registered in the company's register of members, the purchaser of the shares may not vote at meetings of the company. The ability in these circumstances of the purchaser to direct the vendor of the shares as the registered member to vote in company meetings in accordance with his or her wishes, is not an effective protection of the purchaser's rights. Accordingly, unless the purchaser of the shares can obtain his or her registration as the shareholder, the potential purchaser would be advised to withdraw from the transaction.

1 See Chapter 2, para 2.58 onwards and in particular para 2.60 where the power of directors to refuse to register share transactions is considered.

## PARTNERSHIPS

**3.31** The member of a family partnership may seek to sell his partnership share to a third party in order to raise the funds necessary to satisfy a financial provision order. This is not a particularly attractive investment for a potential purchaser. An assignment of a partnership share, in the absence of contrary agreement between the parties to the assignment and the other partners, does not make the assignee a partner in the business. The effect of an assignment therefore, is usually to vest in the assignee the assignor's right to his or her share of the partnership's assets and the right to participate in a share of the profits.

**3.32** Section 31 of the Partnership Act 1890 provides that:

'An assignment by any partner of his share in the partnership, either absolute or by way of mortgage or redeemable charge,[1] does not, as against the other partners, entitle the assignee, during the continuance of the partnership, to interfere in the management or administration of the partnership business or affairs or to require any accounts of the partnership transactions, or to inspect the partnership books, but entitles the assignee only to receive the share of the profits to which the assigning partner would otherwise be entitled, and the assignee must accept the account of profits agreed to by the partners.'

1 Thus this section also applies where a partner seeks to mortgage or pledge his partnership share as security for a loan which may have been obtained for the purposes of meeting the obligations of a financial provision order.

**3.33** The rights of an assignee of a partnership share as regards any involvement in the day-to-day running of the partnership are, by virtue of the above provision, therefore severely restricted. An assignee has a right to any profits which would have accrued to the assignor. However, he or she has no control over the partnership assets per se. In receiving the share of the profits he or she is obliged to accept the partners' accounts which determine such profits unreservedly.

**3.34** Furthermore, if partners in good faith alter the profit-sharing ratios of their business, any assignee of a partnership share may receive a lesser share of the profits of the business than he would otherwise have obtained. This remains so even though he had no influence over their decision. It would also seem that increasing salary payments to partners with a corresponding reduction of profits that would otherwise be available for distribution in respect of each partnership share, cannot be questioned by an assignee of a partnership share.[1] Such an arrangement could be questioned by an assignee of a partnership share, where the arrangement was improper, fraudulent, or designed solely to reduce the amount of profits otherwise payable to the assignee. In other words the assignee only has a limited right to protect his own interests.

1 In *Re Garwood's Trusts* [1903] 1 Ch 236, the partners received salaries as part of a new arrangement for the partners to take a supervisory role in the business in order to stop pilfering. Such an arrangement may be said to be a management decision based on good faith. It would reduce thefts from the business and, in the long term, increase profits. This appeared to be the basis of the court's decision that the assignee of a partnership share had therefore to accept the reduced profits disclosed by the partner's accounts.

**3.35** Where the partnership is in dissolution, the position of the assignee is governed by s 31(2) of the Partnership Act 1890, the section provides that:

'In case of a dissolution of the partnership, whether as respects all the partners or as respects the assigning partner, the assignee is entitled to receive the share of the partnership assets to which the assigning partner is entitled as between himself and the other partners, and, for the purposes of ascertaining that share, to an account as from the date of dissolution.'

## MATRIMONIAL DISPUTES – FAMILY COMPANY DIRECTORS/SHAREHOLDERS/SPOUSES

**3.36** The principal shareholders in a family company may comprise shareholders/directors who are also man and wife. A breakdown in the domestic sphere may have severe repercussions in the shared business enterprise and vice versa. If the business relationship breaks down, then an aggrieved spouse may have recourse to a number of remedies. These may include seeking to have the company wound up, or relief under s 459–461 of the Companies Act 1985.[1] Nevertheless issues of family law and company law will overlap.[2]

1 These remedies have been considered in Chapter 5, para 5.37.
2 In the case of *Poon v Poon* [1994] 2 FCR 777, [1994] 2 FLR 857, Thorpe J was particularly concerned to emphasise that the Family Division of the High Court should retain jurisdiction over disputes which relate either to the function or control of a family company. Nevertheless it should be noted that the case concerned a company in which all the shareholders were related by blood or marriage. It may not be so easy for the Family Division to maintain exclusive jurisdiction in respect of companies where a majority, but not all the members, are so connected.

**3.37** In the case of *Nurcombe v Nurcombe*,[1] a husband and wife held 66% and 34% respectively of the issued share capital of the company. The wife initiated proceedings in the Family Division of the High Court which preceded an action taken by her in respect of the family company. The court granted the wife a divorce in the matrimonial proceedings. The wife became aware, during the divorce proceedings, of an allegation that her husband had diverted a lucrative contract from the family company to another company. The husband had a controlling interest in this other company and would therefore benefit proportionately from this action. The wife sought both maintenance and a lump sum payment in the matrimonial proceedings. The lump sum payment was intended to compensate her for losses sustained by the family company, and therefore indirectly herself in the guise of director/shareholder, and which arose as a consequence of the loss of the lucrative contract to the family company.

1 [1985] 1 All ER 65, [1985] 1 WLR 370, CA.

**3.38** The wife also sought to conduct a derivative action as a minority shareholder[1] of the family company, subsequent to the divorce proceedings. The basis and purpose of this action was to make the husband, as the director/majority shareholder of the family company, liable for the alleged loss of the lucrative contract to the company. The derivative action was dismissed both at first instance and in the Court of Appeal. The Family Division had, in assessing the lump sum payment it had granted to the wife, taken into consideration the profit that the husband, through the medium of the other company was likely to make by virtue of the lucrative contract. Accordingly, the court at first instance and the Court of Appeal had no difficulty in holding that it was inequitable to permit the derivative action to proceed against the husband as director/shareholder of the family company. The wife would not be permitted, having knowledge of the material facts of the husband's conduct, to initiate one action, ie the derivative action in the guise of a shareholder/director, when she had previously sought a remedy in matrimonial proceedings which had already compensated her for the loss she had allegedly suffered as a shareholder. In this case, she had effectively been put to an election, to choose to pursue one out of alternative causes of action, arising from the same facts.

1 See Chapter 5 for a consideration of the nature of these forms of action.

**3.39** Since the corporate action was a derivative action, and therefore the family company's action, it was argued by the wife that there could be no question of election, since the parties in the respective actions, ie derivative and matrimonial, were different. The first instance court and the Court of Appeal were, however, prepared to pierce the corporate veil of the company,[1] and determine that the corporate action was in essence the wife's action. The court was not simply prepared to allow the wife to be compensated twice for what was essentially a single alleged loss, albeit sustained in two separate capacities.[2]

1 This doctrine empowers the court to ignore the separate corporate personality of a company, and to have regard only to the members and/or officers of the company. See Prime & Scanlan *The Law of Private Limited Companies* (Butterworths 1995.) Chapter 2.
2 This situation could not have arisen if the business had been carried on as a family partnership, since the respective separate and joint estates of the parties would not have been regarded by the courts as being distinct in the first instance. The action of the husband would have damaged the interests and estate of the partnership, and therefore the estate and interests of the wife.

CONCLUSION

**3.40** It would seem that a spouse, in cases similar to that of the wife in *Nurcombe v Nurcombe*, will only be put to an election, where both parties to the divorce are aware of all the material facts before any proceedings are initiated by the spouse, or at least before one of the actions although initiated, has not been effectively concluded.

CIRCUMSTANCES IN WHICH THE COURT MAY NOT GRANT A LUMP SUM ORDER

**3.41** In concluding this part of the chapter, consideration should be given to the situations where the court may refuse to grant a lump sum order to a spouse. It has been held by the courts that they will not make such an order if the consequence would be to deprive the payer of his or her livelihood. This has been the case where a partner would have to realise the entirety of his partnership share, having no other property or means of maintaining themselves.[1] Furthermore, a lump sum order may not be appropriate where the payer's wealth is entirely locked up in assets which cannot be readily be sold in order to raise the required capital to satisfy the order. This may be the case where the assets are shares in a family company, and in particular, a minority interest.[2] However, it must be emphasised that the granting of a lump sum order will usually be ordered by a court if it is more valuable to the payee than periodical payments. Accordingly, it is not possible to determine any fixed rules or principles as to when a court will refuse to make such a financial provision order.[3]

1 *P v P* [1978] 3 All ER 70, [1978] 1 WLR 483, CA. The position may be different if the partnership is breaking up or in dissolution. See *B v B* [1989] FCR 146, [1989] 1 FLR 119.

Furthermore, an order should not be made if there is no prospect of the party being able to comply with any order. *Martin v Martin* [1976] Fam 335, [1976] 3 All ER 625, CA.

2 See para 3.30 above. Notwithstanding the above, a lump sum order may be granted if the payer does not produce evidence that he cannot raise the necessary funds by borrowing on the security of the relevant assets. See *Newton v Newton* [1989] FCR 521, [1990] 1 FLR 33, CA. For a consideration of the whole issue of disclosure and discovery and production of documents in matrimonial proceedings involving the family business see Coopers & Lybrand and Collyer-Bristow *Divorce and the Family Business* (Jordans, 1997) Chapter 3.

3 *Jones v Jones* [1971] 3 All ER 1201 at 1206, CA per Davies LJ.

**3.42** Lump sum payments may be paid in instalments, may be secured, and may be subject to interest. Payment by instalments may allow the family business to absorb any lump sum payment more easily.[1]

1 Matrimonial Causes Act 1973, s 23.

### TRANSFER AND SETTLEMENT OF PROPERTY ORDERS

**3.43** Where a matrimonial court grants a decree of divorce, nullity or judicial separation, the court may order either of the parties to the marriage to transfer such property to the other party as specified in the order. Such a transfer may be for the benefit of the transferee or for the benefit of a child of the family. A matrimonial court may also order that either party settle any property for the benefit of the other party, or a child of the family.[1] Although this power is most frequently resorted to by the courts to transfer assets such as the former matrimonial home, it may also be used to order the transfer of property such as investments. Thus the order may be used in respect of property such as shares in a family company. A property transfer order may be made in respect of these forms of investment where it would not be practical to order the sale of those assets in order to provide the capital to satisfy a lump sum order. The jurisdiction of the court would appear to be unrestricted. The court may therefore order an absolute transfer of all of a party's interests in the asset specified in the order or a part thereof. The court has equivalent powers with regard to any settlement it may order.

1 Matrimonial Causes Act 1973, s 24.

### VARIATION OF ANTE-NUPTIAL AND POST-NUPTIAL SETTLEMENTS

**3.44** On the granting of a decree of divorce, nullity or judicial separation the court may make any order:

'... varying for the benefit of the parties to the marriage and of the children of the family or either of them any ante-nuptial and post-nuptial settlement[1] made on the parties to the marriage; and

an order extinguishing or reducing the interest of either of the parties to the marriage under any such settlement;

and the court may make an order ... notwithstanding that there are no children of the family.'[2]

This provision might be used to vary settlements made in contemplation of marriage,[3] where the subject matter of the settlement includes investments such as shares in a family company. The parties to the settlement cannot oust the jurisdiction of the court by agreement. Nor would it seem can the jurisdiction of the court be in any way fettered or restricted by express or implied provision in the agreement or settlement, which seeks to determine how the property is to be held if the marriage is terminated.[4]

1 Including a settlement made by will or codicil.
2 Matrimonial Causes Act 1973, s 24.
3 And where the settlements seek to benefit one or both of the parties to the marriage in the character of a spouse. See *Bosworthick v Bosworthick* [1927] P 64, CA.
4 *Egerton v Egerton* [1949] 2 All ER 238, CA.

## ORDERS FOR THE SALE OF PROPERTY

**3.45** Under s 24A of the Matrimonial Causes Act 1973,[1] where a court makes a secured periodical payments order, a lump sum order, or a property adjustment order, then it may make the following consequential order:

> '. . . a further order for the sale of such property as may be specified in the order, being property in which or in the proceeds of sale of which either or both of the parties to the marriage has or have a beneficial interest, either in possession or in reversion.'

This power is ancillary to, and is dependent on, the court exercising the other powers and making orders relating to the capital assets of the parties to a marriage.

1 Added by s 7 of the Matrimonial Homes and Property Act 1981.

## CONSENT ORDERS

**3.46** The parties to a marriage may, as part of their divorce proceedings,[1] seek to achieve their own negotiated settlement. This is a process that should be welcomed where the one or both of the parties are also members of a family business. Such a financial settlement should ensure that the arrangements relating to the family business are executed with the full and free consent of all involved in that enterprise. It would be wise to have the negotiated settlement incorporated into a court order. The court can therefore make an order on terms agreed. It is important to note that the court retains the power, and the duty, to examine any such negotiated settlement. The court must have regard to the considerations set out in s 25 of the Matrimonial Causes Act 1973 when examining such settlements,[2] and in determining whether to approve such settlements. Nevertheless, in the absence of vitiating factors such as undue influence or mistake, the fact that the parties have arrived at a settlement of their financial affairs, will, especially where the settlement has been negotiated at arms length, and with appropriate independent advice, render such a settlement reasonable.

1 Which includes nullity or judicial separation.
2 See para 3.6 above where these provisions are referred to.

## CONCLUSION

**3.47** The break-up of the family through divorce may have serious financial consequences for the family business. The above text has considered the various forms of financial provision order that may be made in matrimonial proceedings. In most cases the consequences of the making of these orders for the family business are grave, but not fatal. The chapter has considered how the family business may be preserved as an entity following marital breakdown involving one or more of its members, irrespective of whether it is a company or a partnership.[1] Marital breakdown may however, cause such disruption to the family business that it can no longer survive. In these cases it may be sensible for the members of the business to seek to bring it to an end. The mechanisms that may be used to wind-up a business will now be considered. The winding-up of the family business as a company will be outlined first.

1 The comparative advantages in the various circumstances noted in the text of operating the family business as either an incorporated business or a partnership have also been considered.

## LIQUIDATION OF A COMPANY

**3.48** The liquidation or winding-up of a company[1] is the process whereby the company ceases to carry on its business, and where its assets are collected and realised, and its liabilities are fully and finally discharged.[2] In a solvent liquidation, there is a possibility of a net surplus being available for distribution to the members of the company. Any such distribution should be made in accordance with the company's articles of association. There are various solvent liquidation procedures that may be adopted by a family company where family discord, following a divorce involving one or more of the members of the business, dictates that the company should be wound up. These procedures are now considered.[3]

1 The terms are interchangeable.
2 The procedures to be followed where the company is insolvent have been considered in Chapter 6.
3 It must be emphasised that the following procedures could be adopted so as to wind-up a family company for reasons other than marital breakdown. Reasons include the objects of the enterprise not being achieved, or the founding members of the enterprise wishing to retire, and the next generation of the family not wishing to continue the business. The procedures have been considered in the context of marital breakdown because this is a frequent cause of the winding-up of a family business, particularly where the members of the business are the respective spouses. The text will therefore consider some aspects of the law relating to the winding-up of the family company which may not strictly be applicable to a company in which one or more of its members have been involved in divorce or other matrimonial proceedings.

## MEMBERS' VOLUNTARY LIQUIDATION

**3.49** The first company liquidation process for the members of the family company to consider is a members' voluntary liquidation. It can only be invoked in respect of a company which is solvent. It is a pure liquidation procedure. The procedure is initiated by the shareholders of the company when they adopt a special resolution[1] for the voluntary winding-up of the company. However, for the winding-up of the family company to proceed by way of a voluntary liquidation, a majority of the directors of the company must have made a statutory declaration at a meeting of the board of directors that the company is solvent within a five-week period *preceding* the adoption of the resolution.[2] The statutory declaration may be made on the same day as the shareholders' meeting which adopts the resolution to wind-up the company, but it must be made before that meeting begins.[3] Furthermore, the statutory declaration must in any event be filed with the Registrar of Companies before the expiration of 15 days from the date the resolution to wind up the company was adopted.[4]

1 For the nature of a special resolution see para 5.28 and s 378(2) of the Companies Act 1985.
2 Insolvency Act 1986, s 89. If there are only two directors there must be unanimity in making the statutory declaration.
3 Ibid s 89(2)(a).
4 Insolvency Act 1986, s 89(3) and (6), and Sch 10.

**Nature of declaration**

**3.50** The statutory declaration must state that the directors who made it have conducted a full inquiry into the affairs of the company. Furthermore, the declaration must state that in their opinion, the company will be able to meet its obligations in full within a specified period after the commencement of the winding up. This period must not exceed 12 months.[1] Where the family company is being wound-up as a consequence of marital breakdown, and the financial provision following that breakdown is not the result of a negotiated settlement,[2] it may not be possible to predict the effects of any financial provision orders that may be made by the courts in any matrimonial proceedings. In those circumstances, it may not be possible to calculate the effects of such orders on the financial position of the company. Accordingly, in these cases it may not be possible to make the statutory declaration. The company cannot therefore be wound-up on the basis of a members' voluntary winding-up.[3]

1 Insolvency Act 1986, s 89(1).
2 See para 3.46 above for a consideration of the nature and effects of a negotiated settlement of financial provision in connection with a marital breakdown, and the effects of such an agreement on the family business.
3 See para 3.58 below.

**3.51** Subject to the above, if the directors can make the statutory declaration, they must also ensure that the declaration sets out the company's assets and liabilities as at a given date. This date should be as near as is practicable to the date of the making of the declaration. A director making a declaration of solvency without reasonable grounds for any opinions expressed therein commits an offence.[1] If the debts of the family company are not fully paid within the specified period, then the directors who made the declaration are presumed not to have had reasonable grounds for making the declaration.[2]

1 Insolvency Act 1986, s 89(2)(b).
2 Ibid s 89(4) and (5), and Sch 10.

**3.52** The importance of the directors' declaration of solvency lies in the fact that if no declaration is made,[1] then the liquidation of the company can only proceed as a creditors' voluntary liquidation procedure. This form of liquidation is noted below.[2]

1 See para 3.49 above.
2 See para 3.58 below.

### Resolution for voluntary winding up

**3.53** Although as a general rule, for a members' voluntary winding up to commence, the members must adopt a special resolution that the company be wound up, there are situations where these requirement can be dispensed with. In these exceptional circumstances the company may be put into voluntary liquidation by the adoption of an extraordinary or even an ordinary resolution to that effect.[1] This can happen in the following circumstances:

(a) the company cannot continue in business because of its liabilities.[2] In this case the family company will probably become insolvent, and the winding up of the company will therefore generally proceed as a creditors' voluntary winding up;

(b) if the articles of association of the company provide that the company shall cease on the expiration of a specified time, or occurrence of an event to carry on its affairs, and that period has expired, or the event occurred.[3] A winding-up in these cases will usually be by a members' voluntary winding-up.[4]

1 For the nature of such forms of resolution see Chapter 5, para. 5.28. See also the Companies Act 1985, s 378.
2 Insolvency Act, s 84(1)(c). This may be the situation following a marital breakdown involving one or more of the members of the family company.
3 The articles of association cannot provide that a winding-up of the company will take place under any of the above circumstances without the adoption of a resolution.
4 A winding-up in this case will be a rare event, and almost inconceivable as a consequence of a marital breakdown affecting one or more of the members of the family company.

### Appointment of a liquidator

**3.54** In the case of a members' voluntary winding up of a family company, the shareholders in a general meeting must appoint one or more liquidators.[1] The appointment of a liquidator may, and will usually be made at the meeting at which the resolution to wind up the company was adopted. No notice is then required to be given of the intention to propose a resolution to appoint a liquidator.[2]

1 Insolvency Act 1986, s 91(1).
2 *Re Trench Tubeless Tyre Co* [1900] 1 Ch 408, CA.

**3.55** As a general rule, the appointment of a liquidator of the company will result in the abrogation of the authority of the directors and the authority and powers that they may otherwise have exercised in respect of the company are vested in the liquidator. However, the members of the company in general meeting, or the liquidator, may permit the exercise of some of these powers by the directors.[1]

1 Insolvency Act 1986, s 90(2).

**3.56** The shareholders must try to appoint a liquidator soon after the adoption of the resolution to wind up the company. If they fail to do so, any exercise by the directors of their powers will constitute an offence.[1] However, the directors may even in the above circumstances, have limited powers to dispose of company assets if they are of rapidly diminishing value.

The directors may exercise their powers in order to protect the assets of the company.[2]

1 Insolvency Act 1986, s 114.
2 Ibid s 114(3).

**3.57** The above liquidation procedure could be used by the members of the family company to wind-up the enterprise as a consequence of marital breakdown involving one or more of its members, where the marital discord and consequential financial adjustments render the continued operation of the business impracticable. Nevertheless, this form of liquidation requires the members and directors to follow strict procedures and to satisfy stringent conditions, in particular that the company is solvent. This may not prove to be the case in situations where a director/shareholder is the subject of a financial provision order, which may require the sale or transfer of shares in the company. If there is any doubt as to the solvency of the company, it should be wound-up under a creditors' voluntary liquidation.

CREDITORS' VOLUNTARY LIQUIDATION

**3.58** The circumstances where a voluntary winding-up of a family company may subsequently proceed as a creditors' voluntary winding-up have been noted above.[1] This form of liquidation procedure is also a form of insolvency procedure. The initiation of this procedure does not require court sanction or approval. The unsecured creditors[2] of the company may, under this form of liquidation procedure, have the right to appoint a liquidator of the company. They may also appoint a liquidation committee, whose function is to assist the liquidator and to receive reports on the progress of the liquidation. The shareholders are not in these cases stripped of all control over the liquidation process. They may make representations concerning the appointment of the liquidator and may appoint members to the liquidation committee. However, where a liquidator has been nominated by the shareholders, in what is a creditors' voluntary winding-up of the company, then the liquidator's powers are limited. The liquidator may not in these cases exercise his powers as a liquidator unless and until a meeting of the company's unsecured creditors has been called. If the liquidator acts in contravention of the above, he commits an offence.[3] At the meeting of the unsecured creditors, the creditors may displace the liquidator nominated by the shareholders and nominate a new liquidator. The latter will then be appointed unless the court directs otherwise.[4]

1 See paras 3.52 and 3.57.
2 The unsecured creditors may seek the winding-up of the company as a consequence of the company having to come to terms with the financial consequences of a divorce settlement involving one or more of its director/shareholders. Clearly the procedure may be invoked because the company is simply unable to pay its debts. For a consideration of insolvency procedures in general see Chapter 6.
3 Insolvency Act 1986, s 166.
4 Ibid s 100.

**Liquidation committee**

**3.59** The creditors may appoint a liquidation committee in a creditors' voluntary liquidation of a company. They may not appoint more than five persons

50  *Divorce and the family business*

to the committee. Five more persons may be appointed to the committee by the shareholders, although these appointments are subject to veto by the creditors.[1]

> 1 Unless the court orders otherwise (s 101). The court may appoint another person to the committee in place of any party who initially appointed has been the subject of a veto.

**3.60** In addition to assisting the liquidator in his functions and to supervise those functions, the liquidation committee has particular powers, which include[1] the power to:

(a) sanction a proposal by the liquidator; to
 (i) pay any class of creditors in full,
 (ii) make any compromise or arrangement with creditors,
 (iii) compromise any claim the company has against others[2]
(b) sanction the sale of the company's business to another company in exchange for shares in the latter company;[3]
(c) sanction the continuation of the powers of the director of the company;[4]
(d) approve payment of the expenses of the statement of affairs to the liquidator;[5]
(e) approve payment of the expenses of the first meeting of creditors to the liquidator;[6]
(f) settle the liquidator's remuneration;[7]
(g) receive reports from the liquidator, and inspect the liquidator's financial records;[8]
(h) sanction dealings between committee members and the company;[9]
(i) sanction the distribution by the liquidator of the assets of the company in kind to creditors.[10]

It should be noted that the liquidator must notify the committee if he disposes of any company assets to a person connected with the company.[11] The liquidator in a voluntary liquidation of a company, must get in and realise the assets of the company and distribute the proceeds to the company's creditors. If there is a surplus, this must be distributed to the shareholders. The order of application of the assets follows the rules of priority prescribed in a compulsory liquidation, which are considered in Chapter 6.[12]

> 1 The powers listed below are not exhaustive, but have been set out as being those most applicable to the family company. Many of these powers could be exercised by the liquidation committee in order to give effect to financial provision orders or settlements involving one or more of the directors/shareholders of the company.
> 2 Insolvency Act 1986, s 165(2)(b) and Sch 4, paras 1–3.
> 3 Ibid s 110.
> 4 Insolvency Act 1986, s 103.
> 5 Insolvency Rules 1986, r 4.38(4) (as amended by SI 1995/586).
> 6 Ibid r 4.62(4).
> 7 Insolvency Rules 1986, r 4.127.
> 8 Ibid rr 4.155, 4.168 and see the Insolvency Regulations 1986, SI 1986/1994, reg 27(2).
> 9 Insolvency Rules 1986, r 4.170.
> 10 Ibid r 4.183.
> 11 Insolvency Act 1986 s 165. See s 166 for a definition of the concept of the connected person.
> 12 Para 6.75.

COMPULSORY LIQUIDATION

**3.61** A company may be forced into compulsory liquidation as a consequence of marital breakdown involving one or more of its members. This will not be as a direct consequence of the financial provision made by the relevant member, since the assets of the company are distinct from that of the shareholder, but because the marital breakdown begins the process whereby the company can no longer operate profitably.[1] This form of liquidation is considered in Chapter 6.

> 1 This may be a ground for seeking to have the company wound-up under the just and equitable ground see below and Chapter 6.

CIRCUMSTANCES IN WHICH A COMPANY MAY BE WOUND UP

**3.62** A family company following marital discord between its members, may also be wound up as a consequence by order of the court if:

(a) the company has by special resolution resolved that the company be wound up by the court;[1]
(b) the company does not commence trading or carrying on its business within a year from its incorporation, or it suspends its business for a whole year;[2]
(c) the court is of the opinion that it is just and equitable that the company should be wound up.[3]

This last ground is frequently invoked as a reason for winding-up a company by the directors/shareholders of the family company when the relationship between these individuals has broken down. It is a ground frequently resorted to by the members of a company, and is not limited to cases where the breakdown of the relationship of the members is due to marital difficulties between the shareholders.[4]

> 1 Insolvency Act 1986, s 122(1)(a).
> 2 Ibid s 122(1)(d).
> 3 Insolvency Act 1986, s 122(1)(g).
> 4 See Chapter 5, para 5.5 where this ground is considered in the context of protection of minority shareholders.

**3.63** The purpose and function of the liquidator in a compulsory winding-up is the same as that of the liquidator in a voluntary liquidation, and has been considered above.[1]

> 1 Para 3.54 onwards.

THE APPOINTMENT OF A PROVISIONAL LIQUIDATOR

**3.64** After the presentation of a petition to the court for the compulsory winding up of a company, but before disposal of the petition by the court, any person who could have petitioned for the compulsory liquidation of the company, may apply to the court for the appointment of a provisional liquidator. This procedure is applicable to both solvent and insolvent companies. The appointment of a provisional liquidator is not a liquidation procedure. In essence, the purpose of such an appointment is for the provisional liquidator to take control of the company's assets and to preserve the status quo, pending the court's decision on whether to grant the petition to liquidate the company.

## WINDING UP OF COMPANY: COMMENCEMENT

**3.65** A voluntary winding up of a company is deemed to commence at the time of the passing of the resolution to that effect.[1] Where a petition for winding-up of a company is subsequently presented and a winding-up order made, although the company is already in voluntary liquidation, the winding-up of the company is still deemed to have commenced from the date of the adoption of the resolution for the voluntary winding-up of the company.[2]

1 Insolvency Act 1986, s 86.
2 Ibid s 129(1).

**3.66** The general rule is that the date of commencement of a compulsory winding up, is the day the petition was presented.[1] A company subject to compulsory liquidation goes into liquidation when the order to that effect is made by the court. In the case of a voluntary winding up, the company goes into liquidation from the date of adoption of the resolution to that effect.[2]

1 Insolvency Act 1986, s 129(2).
2 Ibid s 247(2).

## DISSOLUTION

**3.67** On the completion of the winding-up of the company, it remains only for the company to be dissolved. The dissolution of the company is the process whereby the Registrar of Companies removes the company from the register. This is in effect the death of the company and its corporate personality. There are a number of ways in which a family company may be dissolved.[1] However, only the ways in which a company may be dissolved following liquidation will be considered below.

1 For further details see Prime & Scanlan *The Law of Private Limited Companies* (Butterworths, 1995) Chapter 23.

### On completion of voluntary liquidation

**3.68** The final stages in the voluntary winding up of a company begin with the filing with the Registrar of Companies of the liquidator's account of the winding up. In addition, a record that a final meeting was held, or summoned but not held due to it being inquorate, should also be filed.[1] On receipt of the above, the Registrar must register them. A notice of the fact of receipt of the above must be published by the Registrar in the Gazette.[2] The company is dissolved three months from the date of registration.[3]

1 Insolvency Act 1986, s 94(3)–(5), s 106(3)–(5).
2 Companies Act 1985, s 711(1).
3 Unless the court orders deferment of dissolution, see s 202(2)–(3), following application by an interested party for deferment under s 201(1).

### Compulsory winding up

**3.69** The liquidator must summon a final meeting of the company's creditors[1] on completion of the compulsory winding-up of the company. He must notify the Registrar if the meeting was held, or if it was summoned but was inquorate.[2] The Registrar must register the notice relating to the holding or summoning of the final meeting. The company is dissolved three months from that date.[3]

1 Insolvency Act 1986, s 146.
2 Ibid s 172(8).
3 Unless there is an application for deferment of dissolution, or the court so directs, s 205(1)–(4).

## THE FAMILY PARTNERSHIP WINDING UP

**3.70** The partnership, unlike the company, is not an entity which is distinct from its members. Accordingly, a financial provision order made against one of the members of the partnership is more likely to bring about the winding up or dissolution of the partnership. The grounds upon which a partnership may be wound up following marital breakdown will now be considered. It must however be noted that these grounds can be used to dissolve a partnership in cases other than marital discord involving one or more of the partners.

### Dissolution under the Partnership Act 1890

**3.71** A partner may subject his partnership share to a charging order in order to raise the finance to satisfy the obligation under a financial provision order. Section 33(2) of the Partnership Act 1890 provides that:

> 'A partnership may, at the option of the other partners, be dissolved if any partner suffers his share of the partnership property to be charged under this Act for his separate debt.'

**3.72** It would appear that, by virtue of this sub-section, the option to dissolve the partnership must be exercised by the unanimous consent of the partners, excluding of course, the partner whose share is the subject of the charging order. The option must be exercised within a reasonable time after the relevant partnership share has been charged. The option would also appear to be incapable of being withdrawn, once it is communicated to the partner whose partnership share is charged.[1] The dissolution of the partnership takes place on the date when the option is exercised. This is a major difference between a partnership and a company. The assignment of a member's shares in a company does not give rise to an automatic statutory right for the other members of the company to seek the dissolution of the company.

1 *Scarf v Jardine* (1882) 7 App Cas 345, HL.

### Dissolution by order of the court

**3.73** A family partnership may be dissolved by order of the court under s 35 of the Partnership Act 1890. The grounds upon which the court may order the dissolution of a partnership under this provision, and which may be applicable to cases involving marital discord or breakdown are:

*(a) Breach of partnership agreement and destruction of mutual confidence;*[1]

This provision constitutes two separate grounds upon which a partnership may be dissolved. The second ground is relevant to situations concerning marital breakdown involving one or more of the partners. Where both parties to a divorce are also partners in the family partnership, the conduct giving rise to the matrimonial proceedings may constitute misconduct on the part of one of the partners, which would destroy the mutual confidence between the partners. The continuance of the partnership is therefore rendered impracticable.[2]

1 Partnership Act 1890, s 35(d).
2 *Re Yenidje Tobacco Co Ltd* [1916] 2 Ch 426, CA.

*(b) Partnership carried on at a loss;*[1]

The need to make provision for a financial provision order may put such financial pressures on the separate estate of a partner that it affects the partner's share in the partnership joint estate. The consequence of this may be that the partnership can never be operated at a profit. In these cases, it may be advisable to seek the dissolution of the partnership under the above provision. This ground can only be invoked where the partnership is practically incapable of ever running at a profit, and cannot be used simply because the divorce settlement has caused temporary financial difficulties for the partnership.

1 Partnership Act 1890 s 35(e).

*(c) The just and equitable ground;*[1]

This ground is considered within the context of minority protection in Chapter 5.[2] There would appear to be no legal objection to using this ground in appropriate circumstances to dissolve a partnership which has been effectively destroyed by marital discord.

1 Partnership Act 1890, s 35(f).
2 Para 5.23.

## DISSOLUTION BY NOTICE

**3.74** A family partnership which has been made into an impracticable business enterprise may be dissolved by the serving of a notice of dissolution between the partners.

**3.75** The notice may be served in accordance with the terms of the partnership agreement or any provisions in the Partnership Act 1890. The partnership agreement will usually prescribe that the matters noted above are grounds for service of a notice of dissolution. The only qualification is that the serving of the notice must be done in good faith, and must not constitute an action which is motivated solely from the desire to secure a personal advantage for the partner or partners serving the notice. In such cases the notice will not be upheld by the courts.[1]

1 *Walters v Bingham* [1988] 1 FTLR 260.

## WINDING UP OF PARTNERSHIP

**3.76** Although a partnership has been dissolved, the authority of the partners continues, but only for the purposes of winding-up the partnership. There are a number of problems that arise following the dissolution of the partnership from whatever cause. One of the principal problems is that of post-dissolution profits. A partnership, unlike a company, is first dissolved and the assets or 'estate' of the partnership are then distributed. In this regard, the partnership is similar to an individual. The 'death' of the partnership, like the death of an individual, precedes the administration or distribution of the estate.

### Post-dissolution profits

**3.77** Partners engaged in post-dissolution transactions, pending the winding-up of the partnership's affairs are entitled to a share in any profits, in accordance with any agreed profit-sharing scheme.[1] This principle is subject to contrary provision made by order of the court. The right to post-dissolution profits may be excluded by the express or implied agreement of the partners and former partners.

1 Partnership Act 1890, s 42. This provision is more fully considered in Chapter 4 concerning the death of a partner in a family partnership.

## DISTRIBUTION OF PARTNERSHIP ASSETS AND ADJUSTMENT OF PARTNERSHIP ACCOUNTS

**3.78** Before a partnership can be wound-up, the partnership accounts must be settled and completed, so as to reflect the rights and obligations of all the partners. In settling accounts between the partners after a dissolution of the partnership, s 44 of the Partnership Act 1890 (which can be excluded by provisions to the contrary in the partnership agreement) provides the following rules:

(a) losses, including losses and deficiencies of capital, must be paid first out of profits, next out of capital, and lastly, if necessary, by the partners individually in the same proportions in which they were entitled to share profits;
(b) the assets of the firm, including the sums, if any contributed by the partners to make up losses or deficiencies of capital, shall be applied in the following manner and order:
  (i) in paying the debts and liabilities of the firm to persons who are not partners;
  (ii) in paying to each partner pro rata what is due from the firm to him for advances as distinguished from capital;
  (iii) in paying to each partner pro rata what is due from the firm to him in respect of capital;
  (iv) the ultimate residue, if any, shall be divided among the partners in the same proportions in which profits are divisible.

**3.79** The effect of the above provisions is that losses must be borne by the partners in the same proportions in which they share the profits of the business, as determined by the partnership agreement. If after discharge of the partnership assets in satisfaction of the obligations listed in (b)(i)–(iii) above,[1] there is a residue, any residue can be distributed to the partners in accordance with the terms of the partnership agreement which prescribe the right of each partner to share the profits of the partnership.

1 If, at any of these three stages, there are insufficient partnership assets to satisfy the burdens so prescribed, any deficiency must be treated as a loss, as in (a) above, and must therefore be borne by the partners in accordance with that provision.

**3.80** The situation is more complicated where the partners have not contributed capital to the partnership in equal shares, but they have nevertheless conducted the business on the basis of the equal sharing of profits and losses. In those cases, any *loss* relating to capital must, as a general principle, be shared between the partners equally, as with any other loss. Furthermore, any assets must be distributed so as to ensure that capital losses are equally shared between all partners.[1]

1 Partnership Act 1890, s 24(1).

**3.81** Section 44 is subject to contrary agreement of the partners. Thus, the partnership agreement may provide that any surplus partnership assets are to be distributed in accordance with the capital contribution of each partner or with the agreed profit-sharing ratios prescribed in the partnership agreement. Losses would therefore be borne on any agreed basis.[1]

1 *Wood v Scoles* (1866) 1 Ch App 369.

## THE RULE IN *GARNER v MURRAY*

**3.82** The above assumes that in the winding-up of the partnership and its final distribution of the partnership assets, all the partners are solvent, and that profits and losses are to be shared equally between the partners. The situation where one of the partners is insolvent[1] was considered in the case of *Garner v Murray*.[2] The court held, in this case, that where s 44 applied to the final settlement of a partnership account, that even where a partner was insolvent, the solvent partners were not compelled to make good any shortfall in capital resulting from the inability of the insolvent partner to contribute to the final account. It is inevitable that there will be a deficiency in capital available for final distribution to the partners. The *solvent* partners will nevertheless contribute their shares of any capital losses in accordance with the prescribed profit-sharing ratio. Ultimately, they will receive any capital thus accumulated, pro rata in accordance with their original capital contributions. Any deficiencies in capital are therefore borne by all the partners, pro rata, in relation to their capital contributions to the partnership, and not in equal shares.

1 The insolvency may have arisen as a consequence inter alia of a marital breakdown.
2 [1904] 1 Ch 57.

## INSOLVENT PARTNERSHIPS

**3.83** Where a partnership and/or its partners are, as a consequence of marital discord, made insolvent, the provisions relating to insolvent partnerships will govern the winding-up of that partnership. These matters are considered in Chapter 6.

CONCLUSION

**3.84** The close relationships that exist between the members of a family business, irrespective of whether that business is a company or a partnership, generally mean that a divorce or any marital discord involving the members will be most likely to have severe consequences for the business. Apart from the emotional and practical difficulties that will be faced by the members of the business faced with such problems, the financial consequences of a partner or shareholder having to meet the commitments of a financial provision order, may ultimately force the business into either solvent or insolvent liquidation. The partnership is a business entity which, unlike the company, is not distinct from its members. The financial burdens faced by a partner as a consequence of matrimonial proceedings, are more likely to bring about financial difficulties for the partnership, with the likelihood of the winding-up of the partnership. The company, at least in legal theory, is a business medium which is more likely to survive the personal financial embarrassment of a director/shareholder following a divorce settlement or financial provision order. This may be a factor in persuading the members of a family business to operate their business through the medium of the private limited company rather than a partnership.

# Chapter 4

# Death and the family business

**4.1** The family business, be it a partnership or a private limited company, will usually include members of different generations of the same family. The business must be structured so that it can survive the inevitable death of any of its members. Furthermore, the death of a member of the family business may give rise to inheritance problems,[1] and the possibility of the beneficial interest in the business vesting in outsiders. This might cause friction in the enterprise and a fundamental shift in the delicate balance of power between the surviving members of the business. Problems that arise on the death of a shareholder in a family company will be considered first.

1 There will also be tax issues, principally capital gains tax and inheritance tax. The text does not permit a detailed consideration of such matters, but see Chapter 1 and *Tiley & Collison's UK Tax Guide*, Parts III, IV and VIII.

DEATH AND THE FAMILY COMPANY

**4.2** The law will cause shares in a family company to be transferred if a shareholder dies. On the death of a shareholder in a family company, the shares are transmitted to his personal representatives. Section 187 of the Companies Act 1985 provides that production of the grant of probate, or letters of administration of the estate, must be accepted by the company as sufficient evidence of the grant, notwithstanding any contrary provision in the articles of association. However, whether the personal representatives can actually be registered as members of the company depends on the articles of association of the particular company. Section 183(3) of the Companies Act 1985, provides that a personal representative may transfer shares in a company, even though he is not registered as the holder.[1] Where Table A applies to a family company, a party becoming entitled to shares in the relevant company on a death may elect either to become a shareholder or to have another party registered as the transferee. In either case, the decision takes effect as a decision to transfer shares by a member of the company. It operates as if death had not occurred. Accordingly, any such election by a personal representative has the effect of triggering any pre-emption provisions which may be prescribed by the articles of association.[2]

1 Section 459(2) (ibid) should also be noted. Section 459 provides that a party to whom shares have been transmitted by operation of law may apply to the court for relief where the affairs of the company are being carried out in a manner that it is unfairly prejudicial to the interests of a (particular) shareholder. The action may be maintained where the directors unreasonably and

unfairly refuse to register a share transfer. In extreme cases an aggrieved party may seek to have the company wound up on the just and equitable ground under s 122(1)(g) of the Insolvency Act 1986. For the nature of these actions see Chapter 5

2 For the nature and effect of such provisions which are designed to ensure that shares in a family company cannot be transferred to outsiders without the present shareholders being given an opportunity to acquire them see both Chapter 2, para 2.58.

**4.3** The personal representative enjoys the same rights as any other shareholder on being registered as a shareholder in a family company. Where the family company has adopted reg 31 of Table A, the personal representatives will in any event, enjoy the same rights before registration as any other shareholder except the right to attend and vote at a general or class meeting. The personal representatives, pending registration as a member of the company, are entitled to be given notice of any company meeting, that is if the company has adopted reg 38 of Table A.[1]

1 See Chapter 2, para 2.60 where the powers of the directors of the company to refuse to register share transfers are considered.

## DEATH OF A CONTROLLING SHAREHOLDER

**4.4** The death of a controlling shareholder of a company may bring about an unforeseen and undesired change in the balance of power within the company. Where a deceased shareholder who was either the founder of the family business or its managing director has bequeathed his shares[1] in the company to particular individuals, he may thereby determine the future control of the company.[2]

1 And his controlling interest in the company.
2 His will may of course either dispose of his entire shareholding to a third party or an outsider. Conversely, the shares may be distributed in blocks to present shareholders.

**4.5** Where, however, no specific testamentary bequest of a share or shares in a company has been made, or the shares of the deceased shareholder need to be sold by the personal representatives to settle estate debts, then the balance of control within a company may be radically altered in an unforeseen and generally undesired manner. In the case of *Lloyds Bank plc v Duker*.[1] A owned 999 shares out of the 1,000 shares issued by the company. The other share was held by his wife. A died and was survived by his wife. The shares were part of his residuary estate. His wife and his bank were appointed executors on trust, either to sell *or* to retain his residuary estate. One half of the residuary estate was to go to his wife, the other half was to be distributed to other beneficiaries. It was eventually decided that the wife was entitled to 46/80 of the residuary estate. Before distribution of A's estate, the wife died. She left the entirety of her estate, including the 46/80 of A's residuary estate to X, the managing director of the company. X asked the wife's executors to transfer 46/80 of the 999 shares in the company to him. These 574 shares would have made him the majority shareholder. The other beneficiaries of A's residuary estate objected to this proposal. The bank as executors of the wife's and husband's estates, sought guidance from the court. The principal options available to the wife's executors were to transfer the percentage of shares to X as determined by the wife's will, *or* to sell all 999 shares on the open market and distribute the proceeds in accordance with the terms of A's will and the wife's will. In normal circumstances, a beneficiary under a will receives his specific entitlement. Where the entitlement under a will consists of shares in a company, this still remains the normal rule, even if this results in a fundamental change in the parties who hold the controlling interest in the company, and reduces the value of shares held by non-influential minority shareholders.[2]

1 [1987] 3 All ER 193, [1987] 1 WLR 1324.
2 Since the market value of such shares as a minority shareholding is disproportionately low as compared with the controlling shareholding in a private limited and therefore a family company see *Re Weiner's Will Trusts* [1956] 2 All ER 482, [1956] 1 WLR 579.

**4.6** In the *Duker* case the court felt justified in departing from the normal rule. It therefore ordered a sale of the shares on the open market, and the beneficiaries received their entitlement in cash. The rationale behind the ruling was that the unit value of any shares of the company which may have vested in the hands of X, would have been higher than the unit value of the shares vested in the minority. Accordingly, vesting X with the majority shareholding would have resulted in him effectively receiving more than 46/80 of the estate.

**4.7** In this case, the court was aware of the fact that in making the order for the sale of the shares, control of the company might pass to outsiders. The judge, therefore, held that X would be free to purchase any of the shares on the open market sale.

**4.8** The death of a shareholder in a family company may cause severe problems for the other shareholders and for the company itself. However, the company has a separate corporate personality from that of its members which ensures that the estates of the personal representatives of the deceased shareholder remain unaffected by the death, unless they are registered as shareholders in the company.[1] Even if this is the case when the personal representatives either become members of the company for the first time, or they increase their shareholding as a consequence of also being the beneficiaries of the estate of the deceased shareholder, their liability for the debts of the company is limited to their shareholding.[2] Furthermore, the death of a shareholder does not bring the existence of the company to an end. The death of a partner in a family partnership produces very different consequences, both for its members and for the business itself.

1 A relevant issue when the personal representatives are frequently members of both the deceased member's family and shareholders in the family company.
2 Where in most family companies the shares are fully paid, the liability of the shareholders is therefore limited. The liability of directors/shareholders may be extended beyond their liability as shareholders in certain circumstances see Chapter 6, paras 6.88 and 6.90.

DEATH AND THE FAMILY PARTNERSHIP

**4.9** The consequences for a family partnership of the death of a partner principally arise because the partnership unlike a company as a business entity is not distinct from its members. The death of a partner will, subject to contrary provision in the partnership agreement, bring about a general dissolution of the partnership.[1] If the partnership is wound up, the personal representatives of a deceased partner have no right to interfere in the business or to become partners, unless they are also the surviving partners or the partnership agreement provides otherwise.[2] Furthermore, the personal representatives of the deceased partner may, unless the partnership agreement provides otherwise, bring an action to have the partnership wound up.[3] Since the surviving partners have no general right in law to acquire the deceased partner's share at an agreed price, a winding-up may be the only way in which the personal representatives can recover the value of the deceased partner's share. If these options are impractical the personal representatives may have no alternative but to allow the deceased partner's share to remain in the business, and to allow the business to continue. The problems that arise from this course of conduct are set out below.

1 See s 33(1) of the Partnership Act 1890 and also Chapter 2, paras 2.18 and 2.19 which considers, inter alia, how the death of a partner may result in only a technical dissolution of the partnership if the partnership agreement so provides. Any form of dissolution in such cases may be entirely avoided.
2 Such an agreement may be implied by the conduct of the partners.
3 Partnership Act 1890, s 39.

**4.10** In order to allow the partnership share of a deceased partner to remain in the business, the personal representatives need to obtain the full and free consent of the beneficiaries of the deceased partner's estate.[1] Furthermore, even if the beneficiaries agree, the personal representatives would also run the risk of being considered as partners in the business or as being held out as partners to third parties who deal with the partnership.[2] Unless the personal representatives are also existing partners in the family partnership, they may well be forced to seek the immediate dissolution of the partnership because of the liability of being considered a partner. It follows that it is generally not advisable for a partner to be the executor of a fellow partner, since it will place the partner executor in a position where the duties he owes as a partner to the partnership conflict with the duties he owes to the beneficiaries under the will. Nevertheless, such a situation will frequently arise where the partnership is a family partnership, and the partners are generally, if not exclusively, the intended beneficiaries of one another's estates.

1 In the case of many family partnerships, the personal representatives of a deceased partner will also be his or her principal beneficiaries.
2 With the consequence that they and their separate estates will be liable without limit on any such transactions.

**4.11** Although, as a general rule, the personal representatives of a deceased partner cannot interfere in the running of the partnership business, they nevertheless have an interest in the debts owed to, and liabilities of, the partnership.[1]

1 The personal representatives may, in certain circumstances, between dissolution and the winding-up of the partnership seek a share of any post-dissolution profits or interest on the deceased partner's share under s 42 of the Partnership Act 1890 – see para 4.24.

THE CREDITORS OF A PARTNERSHIP

**4.12** A deceased partner's estate remains, as a general principle, liable for debts incurred by the partnership before his death. The estate remains liable, notwithstanding any arrangements or dealings made between the creditors, unless their actions extinguish any liability or their conduct indicates that they have abandoned or lost their rights against the deceased partner's estate.

**4.13** A creditor of the partnership may proceed against a deceased partner's estate to recover any debts incurred by the partnership prior to the death, without proceeding against the surviving partners.[1] It would however, be advantageous for a creditor to add the surviving partners to the action, as the creditor may then proceed against all of the partnership assets in satisfying any judgment obtained. It should be noted that the creditor of a partnership does not rank equally with the deceased partner's separate creditors. Conversely, the separate creditors of the deceased partner have no rights against the deceased partner's partnership share of the partnership assets until the debts of the partnership have been satisfied.[2]

1 *Wilkinson v Henderson* (1833) 1 My & K 582.
2 *Hills v M'Rae* (1851) 9 Hare 297.

## DEBTS INCURRED BY A PARTNERSHIP AFTER A PARTNER'S DEATH

**4.14** As a general principle, a deceased partner's estate is not liable to third parties for any transactions entered into by the surviving partners of the family partnership after the death of the deceased partner.[1] However, the deceased partner's estate remains liable in respect of liabilities incurred by the surviving partners which have been necessarily and properly entered into in order to effect the winding-up of the partnership.

1 *Bagel v Miller* [1903] 2 KB 212.

## PERSONAL REPRESENTATIVES ADMITTED AS PARTNERS

**4.15** Where the personal representatives of a deceased partner are admitted as partners[1] to the family partnership, they will be rendered personally liable for any liabilities incurred by the partnership from the date of admission. They do not however, thereby automatically impose any liability on the deceased partner's estate. Where executors of a deceased partner's estate, leave the deceased's partnership assets within the business without the express authority of the testator,[2] and by implication carry on or permit the surviving partners to carry on the family partnership, they may render that part of the deceased partner's estate subject to any liabilities subsequently incurred by the partnership.[3] This drastic consequence for a deceased partner's estate ensures that executors should not act in this way, unless that action has been specifically and expressly authorised by the deceased partner in his will.[4] Such an express power must be unambiguous in its intent.[5] A deceased partner's partnership share will not incur liability after his death if the relevant assets are retained in the business for a short time, and the personal representatives are admitted as partners for the sole purpose of realising those assets.[6] Furthermore, the testator may have directed that his partnership share be left within the family partnership as a loan to the surviving partners.[7] This presumption as to liability will be rebutted where the executors are also empowered to carry on the business and seek to enforce this power.

1 See para 4.9 above where this issue is considered.
2 *Wightman v Townroe* (1813) 1 M & S 412. For the purposes of this part of the text, personal representatives include both an administrator and an executor.
3 And for which the beneficiaries may have a remedy against the personal representatives.

*The separate creditors of the deceased partner's estate and beneficiaries* 63

4 Or in the case of a family partnership, the personal representatives admitted as partners are also the sole beneficiaries under the deceased partner's will.
5 *Kirkman v Booth* (1848) 11 Beav 273.
6 *Marshall v Broadhurst* (1831) 1 Cr & J 403.
7 With the consequence that the deceased partner's estate is not liable for any liabilities incurred by the partnership subsequent to the death of the partner. But note that if the loan is not to bear interest and the interest is to vary with the profits of the family partnership, then the loan may be perceived as an advance of capital and the deceased partner's estate may remain liable on debts incurred by the partnership subsequent to the death of the deceased partner. See also s 2 of the Partnership Act 1890.

**4.16** Where a surviving partner is appointed as executor of a deceased partner's estate and subsequently carries on the business, the deceased partner's estate will then remain liable for debts and obligations which the partnership has incurred post death. A similar situation arises where the personal representatives have lawful authority to leave the assets of the deceased partner in the family partnership.[1] The assets of the deceased partner's estate are thus rendered available to discharge liabilities incurred by the partnership after his death.

1 In accordance with a provision in the will see para 4.15 above. Cf the situation if there is no such authority, *ex p Garland* (1804) 10 Ves 110.

**4.17** Where the personal representatives of a deceased partner carry on the partnership business in accordance with an express power in the will,[1] or in order to realise the relevant assets, or with the full consent of the beneficiaries,[2] they will then be entitled to an indemnity from the estate for any personal liability they may so incur. The liability of the estate will not, as a general rule, exceed the amount that the deceased left for use in the family partnership business.[3] Although in these circumstances the personal representatives are given a right of indemnity,[4] their creditors remain the creditors of the personal representatives, and are not the creditors of the deceased partner's estate. Accordingly, those creditors only have a right of action against the personal representatives.[5]

1 Or in accordance with a statutory power to postpone the sale of the deceased partner's estate.
2 Who, in the case of a family partnership, may be the same parties as the personal representatives.
3 *Cutbush v Cutbush* (1839) 1 Beav 184.
4 Each personal representative is given a separate right of indemnity *Re Frith* [1902] 1 Ch 342.
5 Although the situation may be different where the deceased's trust fund was created in the will for the purpose of carrying on the partnership business, see *Strickland v Symons* (1884) 26 Ch D 245, CA.

## THE SEPARATE CREDITORS OF THE DECEASED PARTNER'S ESTATE AND BENEFICIARIES

**4.18** The separate creditors of the deceased partner's estate and those beneficially entitled to the estate must seek their share of the estate from the personal representatives. In calculating the size of the estate, the personal representatives will need to decide what proportion of the estate is derived from the testator's share in the partnership.[1] Although, as a general principle, only the personal representatives can seek an account from the surviving partners, an account can also be taken in proceedings for an administration order of the deceased's estate, instituted against the personal representatives, by the deceased's separate creditors, legatees or next of kin. In any action taken by the separate creditors or the beneficiaries of the deceased partner's estate, the court can order a valuation of the share of the partnership that forms part of the estate. Any such valuation will require an account of the deceased partner's entire estate, including his partnership share. Nevertheless, although the position is not entirely free from doubt, the surviving partners cannot be compelled to pay out any sum which is due to the estate. Payment could be enforced in third party proceedings taken by the personal representatives.[2]

1 Unless specifically bequeathed.
2 RSC Ord 16, r 1(1)(b); CCR Ord 12, r 1(1)(b).

**4.19** In exceptional circumstances those beneficially entitled or interested in the deceased partner's estate may institute proceedings directly against the partnership, the surviving partners, and the personal representatives. Such circumstances would include the situation where the personal representatives have acted improperly so as to prevent those entitled or interested in the deceased partner's estate from obtaining their rights and dues under the estate. A legal action could also be taken where the personal representatives are also the partners in the family partnership,[1] or the personal representatives and the surviving partners are in collusion.[2]

1 *Beningfield v Baxter* (1886) 12 App Cas 167, PC.
2 *Alsager v Rowley* (1802) 6 Ves 748.

**4.20** The separate creditors, or those entitled under the deceased partner's estate, have no remedy or right to impeach a bona fide account settled between the personal representatives and the surviving partners.

LOANS TO THE PARTNERSHIP

**4.21** As has been noted above, a deceased partner's partnership share may be left in the partnership business as an interest bearing loan. The personal representatives can then only claim the agreed interest and not a share of the profits derived from the use of the loan by the partnership.[1] The personal representatives will not be held personally liable for any loss to the deceased partner's estate if they have acted properly, and within the scope of their authority vested in them by the deceased partner's will. The separate creditors, legatees, or next of kin, cannot enjoy any effective rights in the partnership share while it is outstanding as a loan. This remains the case even if the partnership share has been lent to the family partnership in breach of trust, unless the surviving partners are aware of the breach of trust.[2]

1 *Vyse v Foster* (1872) 8 Ch App 309.
2 *Stroud v Gwyer* (1860) 28 Beav 130.

**4.22** Where a personal representative, who is also a surviving partner,[1] uses the deceased partner's share in the partnership business without lawful authority, he commits a breach of trust. He is then liable to account to the beneficiaries of the deceased partner's estate for the value of the partnership share, together with interest at a rate of 5%. As an alternative, the parties entitled under the deceased partner's estate may claim any profits which can be attributed to the use of that share. The remedies available in the above circumstances are based on the equitable doctrine of breach of trust. They mirror and complement the remedies available to ex-partners, personal representatives of deceased partners, and those interested in the estate of a deceased partner where a partnership share is used by the family partnership following dissolution, without settlement of an account under the Partnership Act 1890, s 42.[2]

[1] This will be a common occurrence in the case of many family partnerships.
[2] Section 42 is considered within the context of a deceased partner at para 4.24 below.

**4.23** It is therefore advisable that any legal action taken by the beneficiaries of the deceased partner's estate, which involves a claim to profits attributable to the use of the deceased partner's partnership share, should involve the joining of all the surviving partners as parties to the action.[1]

[1] Such an action is advisable, because not all the relevant profits may be in the hands of the personal representatives. A claim for mixed profits and interest will succeed only in exceptional circumstances, see *Heathcote v Hulme* (1819) 1 Jac & W 122. A claim for compound interest is more readily accepted by the courts, see *Vyse v Foster* (1874) LR 7 HL 318 at 346.

**4.24** Where the surviving partners, who are not personal representatives of the deceased partner, are aware that a deceased partner's share has been left in the business, they may be held liable to those beneficially interested in the estate under the terms of s 42 of the Partnership Act 1890. It would seem, by analogy with personal representatives/surviving partners, that partners who are not the personal representatives of a deceased partner, but who are aware that a partnership share has been left in the partnership business in breach of trust, will be liable for any loss sustained by those entitled to or interested in the deceased partner's estate. Proof of knowledge of the breach of trust by the surviving partners will be borne by the parties bringing the action. The standard of proof, however, remains the civil standard of proof.[1]

[1] *Booth v Booth* (1838) 1 Beav 125.

**4.25** It should be noted that by virtue of s 42(2) of the Partnership Act 1890, a personal representative of a deceased partner may not claim a share in the profits of the family partnership earned by the business post death. This is the case where the surviving partners have an option to acquire the former partner's partnership share, and that option is duly exercised, and its terms strictly carried out.[1] Furthermore, the right to claim post death profits under s 42 may be excluded by the express or implied agreement of the partners and former partners. Such an agreement may be inferred from the provisions of the partnership agreement.[2]

[1] *Vyse v Foster* (1874) LR 7 HL 318 at 329.
[2] Thus the partnership agreement may provide that a deceased partner's share in the partnership automatically accrues to the surviving partners. This may be supplemented by a provision in the partnership agreement that the beneficiaries under a deceased partner's will or on intestacy receive the benefits of a life insurance policy taken out by the partnership in favour of the partners, rather than a right to the deceased partner's partnership share. See Chapter 2, para 2.19.

**4.26** In conclusion it must be emphasised that where a personal representative is admitted to a partnership,[1] not in his representative capacity but as a partner in his own right, any profits which accrue to him are his personal property, and not to be regarded as the assets of the deceased partner's estate.[2]

[1] For the procedure governing the admission of a new partner to a family partnership, see Chapter 5, para 5.2.
[2] *Simpson v Chapman* (1853) 4 De GM & G 154.

## BEQUEST OF PARTNERSHIP SHARE

**4.27** A partner may, subject to the terms of the partnership agreement, or the provisions of the Partnership Act 1890, dispose of his partnership share. He may make a disposition of something less than his outright interest in that share to an individual.[1] A bequest does not constitute a nomination, admitting the beneficiary to the partnership. The bequest of a partnership share entitles the beneficiary to the amount due to the partner at the time of his death, and subject to the will and/or partnership agreement, a share of the profits made by the partnership since the death of the partner/testator.

> 1 This situation may arise either because that is the clearly expressed intention of the partner, or because the bequest is ambiguous and is so construed by the courts. See *Re Rhagg* [1938] Ch 828, [1938] 3 All ER 314.

**4.28** A bequest by a deceased partner of his capital in the partnership will therefore include all that was due to him in respect of advances, including undrawn profits credited to the deceased partner's capital account, but restricted to such profits which were withdrawable at will and which would not form part of the partnership's fixed capital. A bequest by a deceased partner of the net profits of his partnership share will only include profits accruing during the continuation of the partnership business.[1] Furthermore, a bequest by a deceased partner of his partnership share of the goodwill does not carry a right for the beneficiary to compel the surviving partners to sell the goodwill of the business, and distribute the proceeds among the partners.[2]

> 1 *Re Lawes-Wittewronge* [1915] 1 Ch 408.
> 2 *Robertson v Quiddington* (1860) 28 Beav 529.

**4.29** Partnership shares cannot be attributed to a particular partnership asset or assets. A bequest, therefore, cannot be made in respect of a particular partnership asset.[1] However, where a deceased partner has also made testamentary legacies for the surviving partners,[2] they can decide either to permit the particular partnership asset to go to the beneficiary or to provide compensation out of their legacies.[3]

> 1 Although it is not out of the question in the case of a family partnership that, subject to payment of the partnership debts out of the partnership assets, effect may be given to such a bequest, as a concession by the surviving partners see *Re Rhagg* [1938] Ch 828, [1938] 3 All ER 314.
> 2 A common occurrence in the case of family partnerships.
> 3 Under the so-called equitable doctrine of election see *Re Gordon's Will Trusts* [1978] Ch 145, [1978] 2 All ER 969, CA.

**4.30** A beneficiary of a deceased partner, who is also a debtor of the estate, may not receive any benefit from the bequest until he has discharged any debts owed to the estate.[1]

> 1 It should be noted that this principle does not apply to a beneficiary who is a partner in the enterprise which itself is indebted to the estate of the deceased see *Turner v Turner* [1911] 1 Ch 716.

**4.31** Where a partner makes a bequest of his partnership share, but subsequently leaves the partnership, and is fully compensated by the former partners, his bequest will be subject to the equitable doctrine of ademption on his death. This doctrine requires that a specific legacy such as a partnership share, must exist at the time of the testator's death. If the property left in the will has been lost, destroyed, exchanged or sold prior to the testator's death, then the bequest is regarded as revoked. However, the doctrine of ademption cannot apply to a bequest of a partnership share while the testator remains a partner, and if he is still a partner at the time of his death. This is irrespective of the degree to which the testator's partnership interests or the nature of his partnership share have been transformed since the date of the making of the will.[1]

1 *Backwell v Child* (1755) Amb 260.

## LIFE INTERESTS

**4.32** In his will, a partner may settle his partnership share on life interest trusts. The rules of equity provide that personal property, which includes a partnership share, may in these circumstances be subject to the doctrine of conversion. The doctrine of conversion states that the property which is subject to the life interest trust should be sold, and the life tenant should receive the income from the proceeds of sale which should be invested by the personal representatives/trustees.[1] This rule may be displaced by a clear contrary intention expressed in the will. However, only such an unambiguous contrary testamentary intent will entitle the life tenant to seek to prevent the conversion of the partnership share.[2] This doctrine of conversion was stated in the case of *Howe v Lord Dartmouth*[3] and does not apply to a life interest in a partnership share under the rules of intestacy.[4] In such cases, the personal representatives can distribute the income arising from the partnership share itself to the life tenant.[5] Any trading losses arising from the continuation of the family partnership by the surviving partners, and which are borne in proportion to the deceased partner's partnership share, must not automatically be satisfied by selling or disposing of the capital invested in the business. Any such practice would prejudice the interests of the remaindermen, and unduly favour the current life tenant.[6]

1 *Howe v Earl of Dartmouth* (1802) 7 Ves 137.
2 *Re Trollope's Will Trusts* [1927] 1 Ch 596. An express power in the will to postpone the sale of the relevant property will not be sufficient to entitle the life tenant to insist that the partnership share remains unconverted.
3 See n 1 above.
4 In such cases, the beneficiary is most likely to be the spouse of the deceased partner.
5 *Re Fisher* [1943] Ch 377, [1943] 2 All ER 615 and the Administration of Estates Act 1925, s 33(5), (7).
6 It would be irrelevant that the life tenant is the surviving spouse of the deceased partner. See *Upton v Brown* (1884) 26 Ch D 588.

**4.33** Unless the will of a deceased partner clearly expresses the contrary intent, then the life tenant of an unconverted partnership share is not entitled to profits attributable to the partnership share prior to the testator's death.[1] Nor, under the same principle, will the life tenant of an unconverted partnership share be entitled to profits attributable to the share and declared after the testator's death, but which were earned, and which should have been declared, before the testator's death. Such profits should fall into the deceased partner's general estate.[2]

1 *Ibbotson v Elam* (1865) LR 1 Eq 188.
2 *Browne v Collins* (1871) LR 12 Eq 586.

## LIFE INTERESTS AND THE FAMILY COMPANY

**4.34** Unlike the family partnership, the family company is not concerned with life interests or trusts of its shares. By virtue of s 360 of the Companies Act 1985 no notice of any trust,[1] express, implied or constructive shall be entered on the register, of a private limited company or be receivable by the Registrar. Where reg 5 of Table applies, the company is not required except by law, to recognise any registered member of the company as holding shares upon any trust. Except as otherwise provided for by the articles of association, the company shall not be bound by, or recognise, any interest in those shares except where the holder is entitled to all legal and equitable interests in the shares. Accordingly, where this provision applies, the company is not liable to the beneficiaries for breach of trust committed by personal representatives/trustees who are the registered shareholders.

1 Including a life interest created in shares or securities of the company.

**4.35** The beneficiary in the above circumstances is not left without any direct action to protect his position. He may do so by means of a stop notice.[1] A stop notice is affected by filing an affidavit disclosing the relevant facts, together with a notice to the court. Office copies are served on the company. The effect of a stop notice is that the company may not register a transfer of the shares or take any other steps prevented by the stop notice until 14 days after the sending of the notice to the person on whose behalf it was filed. However, the stop notice offers limited protection to the beneficiary, because the company must act in accordance with the notice, but the company may treat the personal representative/trustee in all other respects as if he were the outright owner as well as holder of the shares, and in this respect no different from any other registered shareholder.

1 See the Charging Orders Act 1979 and the RSC Ord 50, rr 11–14.

## WINDING UP OF THE FAMILY BUSINESS ON DEATH OF A MEMBER

**4.36** The death of a member of a family business may bring the business to an effective end. This will be the case irrespective of whether the business is run as a company or a partnership. It may however, be the case that the partnership is particularly vulnerable to the death of a partner because of the direct nexus between the partnership as a business and the individual partner. In the case of the death of a partner, the only course of action may be to wind-up the family partnership. The relevant procedures depend on whether the partnership is solvent or insolvent and have been considered elsewhere.[1] Where the presence of a director/shareholder in a family company is a crucial factor in its continued prosperity, it may be unable to survive the death of that individual. In such cases, the separate corporate personality of the company from that of its members is a legal fiction. The death of the director/shareholder may prove the effective end of the company. The only course of action left open to the remaining members is to put the company into liquidation.[2]

1 In the case of an insolvent partnership in Chapter 6, and in the case of a solvent partnership in Chapter 3, within the context of a family partnership wound-up as a consequence of marital discord. These procedures are of course available to the partnership in cases other than marital discord involving the partners, including the death of a partner.

2 See Chapters 3 and 6 where the liquidation procedures that may be available in such cases are considered. The voluntary liquidation procedures considered in Chapter 3 in connection with matrimonial disputes involving the shareholders are also applicable in the cases of the death of a member.

## CONCLUSIONS

**4.37** The death of a member of a family business cannot fail to have a profound effect on that enterprise, although the decision by the surviving members to wind-up the business as a consequence may not be substantially influenced by the form of the business. This chapter has however, illustrated that the death of a member of a family partnership causes particular problems to a partnership which is not shared by the company. Many of these problems arise because the partnership is a business enterprise which has no legal personality distinct from that of its members. This may be a factor which the founding members of a family business should consider when setting up and operating their business. The comparative lack of legal problems that face the family company on the death of one of its directors/shareholders is a factor that may tip the balance in favour of selecting the private limited company as against the partnership as the medium for operating the family business.

# Chapter 5

# Minority protection

THE PARTNERSHIP AND THE MINORITY PARTNER

**5.1** Where the family business is carried on through the medium of a partnership, the issue of the protection of the rights of a minority family partner may be an acute problem. The minority partner must seek to ensure that his interests in the business are not entirely subjugated to those of the majority by recourse to provisions in the partnership agreement or by reference to statutory provision and case law. However, the protection of the interests of the minority partner must not unduly prejudice the day-to-day operation of the partnership. The partnership agreement should therefore be drafted so as to effect a fair and workable balance between these two conflicting aims. A well-drafted partnership agreement should, in effecting this balance, address the following matters.

UNANIMOUS DECISIONS: MAJORITY VOTING

**Admission of a new partner**

**5.2** The admission of a new partner to the family partnership is a potential source of conflict between the existing members of the business. The admission of a son, daughter, niece or nephew of an existing partner to the partnership may produce a willing ally for that partner, and a serious upset in the balance of power. The emotional aspect of sibling rivalry cannot be ignored in these circumstances. The admission of a spouse of a family partner to the partnership may be viewed by other partners as opening family affairs to an outsider.[1] Accordingly, it is sensible for a family partnership agreement to provide that the admission of any new partner is a matter for unanimity with regard to the existing partners.[2] Such a provision gives effect to s 24(7) of the Partnership Act 1890, which requires the consent of all the existing partners to the introduction of a new partner. However, s 24(7) does not prevent the partnership agreement from making provision to the contrary.

1 The potential tax advantages of a partnership employing spouses of partners as opposed to admitting them as partners should be noted. See Chapter 1.
2 See 30 *Forms & Precedents* Form 2, clause 3.

**5.3** A clause in a partnership agreement may prescribe the procedure for admission of a partner,[1] a particularly attractive option in a family partnership agreement. An admission procedure which requires the full and frank disclosure of all relevant matters should help a minority family partner to protect his interests, by restricting the admission of new partners otherwise than in accordance with the general aims and objectives of the partnership agreed by the founding partners. The partnership agreement may also restrict the class of persons who may be admitted as partners. The family partnership agreement may thus restrict the admission of partners to those who are linear descendants of some or all of the founding partners. Such a provision, it is submitted, cannot breach any anti-discrimination legislation. Partners may be given an absolute or qualified veto on the admission of new partners.[2]

1 Including conditions of entry, see *Byrne v Reid* [1902] 2 Ch 735, CA.
2 Conversely where the partnership agreement merely provides that a new partner cannot be admitted without the consent of the existing partners, such consent should not be unreasonably withheld. See *Re Franklin and Swathling's Arbitration* [1929] 1 Ch 238.

PARTNERS' DUTIES

**5.4** A minority partner in a family partnership can be effectively protected from oppressive conduct by the majority, by ensuring that the minority partner is kept fully informed of all partnership activities. The partnership agreement should therefore provide that each partner owes a duty of good faith, must be just and faithful to the other partners and is obliged to make full and frank disclosure of all matters relating to the affairs of the partnership. Although such provisions will be implied in any partnership,[1] express obligations to that effect prescribed in the partnership agreement will it is submitted give a partner the right to seek damages against his co-partners in the event of a breach of any such obligation by a co-partner or co-partners.[2] Furthermore, a breach of any such obligation may constitute a ground for expulsion of the recalcitrant partner.[3] Although expulsion is a drastic remedy it may, as a potential threat, place a restraint on an otherwise irresponsible or oppressive set of partners.

1 *Blisset v Daniel* (1853) 10 Hare 493; *Maddeford v Austwick* (1826) 1 Sim 89; *Law v Law* [1905] 1 Ch 140, CA.
2 On the basis that there has been an actionable breach of covenant.
3 See 30 *Forms & Precedents* Form 2, clause 22.

MANAGEMENT

**5.5** The partnership agreement should provide which partnership decisions may be decided by majority and those that require qualified majority or unanimity. The determination of these issues is an effective guarantee for a minority partner that the partnership will be managed in accordance with the wishes and aspirations of all the partners. In the absence of any such provision in the agreement, s 24(8) of the Partnership Act 1890 provides:

> 'Any difference arising as to ordinary matters connected with the partnership business may be decided by a majority of the partners, but no change may be made in the nature of the partnership business without the consent of all existing partners.'

**5.6** Section 24(8) of the Partnership Act 1980 therefore draws a crucial distinction between so called ordinary matters and those matters which effect changes in the partnership business. Extensive case law has nevertheless failed to give more than a bare outline of the types of situations which will constitute ordinary matters or issues which effect fundamental change in the partnership.[1] Furthermore, what constitutes an ordinary matter must be a question of fact which will depend on the nature of the relevant partnership business and the custom and practice observed by that partnership and by other partnerships engaged in that form of commercial enterprise. A family partnership agreement relating to a family partnership should therefore attempt to define precisely the areas which shall be determined by bare majority, qualified majority or unanimity, thus displacing the operation of s 24(8).

1 *Highley v Walker* (1910) 26 TLR 685.

## UNANIMITY

**5.7** It is suggested that unanimity should be required in respect of the following matters.

### (a) Changes in any provisions in the partnership agreement[1]

**5.8** This will include changes in the management structure which are prescribed in the partnership agreement. It will be common practice for the day-to-day management of the partnership to be entrusted to certain partners, while other partners fulfil the role of a dormant partner. Although a dormant partner may also be a minority partner, it is appropriate in many family partnerships that such a partner should have an effective voice in determining which members of the partnership should run the family enterprise on a daily basis.

1 Section 24(8) of the Partnership Act 1890 merely provides that the business of the partnership cannot be changed without unanimity of the partners.

### (b) The firm's name

**5.9** The partnership name attracts goodwill and is an asset of value to any successful family enterprise. The admission of new family members may subsequently lead to pressure to change the firm name, despite commercial realities which would militate against such a change. The fact that the elder members of the family partnership may wish to retain the firm name for the sake of sentiment and perceived tradition, are factors which cannot be ignored. It may therefore be advisable to provide that the firm name can only be changed by unanimous agreement of the partners.[1]

1 See 30 *Forms & Precedents* Form 2, clause 4.

### (c) Ratification of a partner's activities which fall outside that partner's actual authority

**5.10** Where a partner has acted outside his actual authority and has incurred liability on behalf of the partnership, he may nevertheless bind his co-partners as regards any third parties.[1] A common provision in a partnership agreement is for the partner who has so acted to indemnify his co-partners for any liability incurred by the partnership and the partners. It is possible for the partners to ratify any action of a partner which falls outside the scope of his actual authority, thus nullifying the operation of any indemnity clause. In order to protect the interests of a minority partner, who may not approve of the action of the recalcitrant partner, the partnership agreement should provide that ratification requires the fully informed and unanimous consent of all the partners.

1 Because of the concept of ostensible or apparent authority. For a consideration of the nature of actual and apparent authority of partners see Prime & Scanlan *The Law of Partnership* (Butterworths, 1995) Chapter 6.

## EXPULSION OF A PARTNER

**5.11** It is highly desirable that the family partnership agreement contains provisions allowing for the expulsion of individual partners who commit material breaches of the partnership terms, or on the occurrence of prescribed events.[1] Such prescribed provisions or events could include behaviour on the part of a partner or partners whose conduct is inimical to the interests of a minority partner. The family partnership agreement should therefore provide for the expulsion of 'problem' partners, protecting the interests of the partnership and where appropriate a minority partner, without affecting the continuation of the partnership.

1 See 30 *Forms & Precedents* Form 1 (Formation checklist), para 18. There is no power in the Partnership Act 1890 to expel a partner from the partnership in the absence of an express power in the partnership agreement s 25.

**5.12** The provisions in any family partnership agreement which prescribe the grounds for expulsion of a partner must be drafted with care, since the courts will construe any clause empowering expulsion strictly against the party relying on the clause.[1] Any expulsion clause in a family partnership agreement should specify the minimum number of partners who can invoke such a provision.[2] It is suggested that any expulsion clause in a family partnership should be invoked by a minimum of two partners, although in cases where the partnership is small there would appear to be no practical objection to a single partner being able to invoke such a provision.[3]

1 *Hitchman v Crouch Butler Savage Associates* (1983) 127 Sol Jo 441, CA. Although where a manifest absurdity will result from such a literal approach the courts will construe an expulsion clause so as to avoid such a consequence.
2 See 30 *Forms & Precedents* Form 2, clause 22.1.8. That clause provides that there must be more than one partner seeking to expel another partner.
3 See *Walters v Bingham* [1988] 1 FTLR 260, although the expulsion of a partner from a two partner partnership may be difficult to distinguish from a dissolution of such a partnership.

**5.13** It is submitted that it would be sensible for the expulsion clauses in a family partnership agreement to provide for a partner being expelled to be given written notice of the fact, together with the grounds of expulsion. The partner being expelled should also be given an opportunity to be heard and to contest the proposed expulsion in accordance with the principles of natural justice.[1]

1 Case law is uncertain as to whether the rules of natural justice should be applied to any expulsion procedure. See *Barnes v Youngs* [1898] 1 Ch 414; *Re A Solicitors' Arbitration* [1962] 1 All ER 772, [1962] 1 WLR 353; *Green v Howell* [1910] 1 Ch 495, CA; *Peyton v Mindham* [1971] 3 All ER 1215, [1972] 1 WLR 8. These cases determined that the expulsion procedures did

not have to observe the rules of natural justice, only that the partners seeking to expel a partner acted in good faith. These cases however, involved two partner firms and may be distinguished from cases such as *Barnes v Young* which did require the rules of natural justice to be observed where partners were expelled.

## GOOD FAITH

**5.14** It is clear that a partner or partners in seeking to expel a partner must act in good faith. In *Kerr v Morris*[1] Dillon LJ defined the requirement in the following terms:[2]

> 'Prima facie it may be said, therefore, with some force that, if the other partners are giving the defendant notice of expulsion, they must specify a reason for giving it . . . which must prima facie be a reasonable reason... So it may well be that, apart from the question whether they were bound to afford him a hearing . . . the question . . . will come down to whether they were justified in their honest belief that the trust necessary between partners had been breached by the defendant.'

1 [1987] Ch 90, [1986] 3 All ER 217, CA.
2 Ibid at 111.

**5.15** This judicial view lends force to the argument that in expelling a partner, the other partner(s) should seek to apply the rules of natural justice to the expulsion procedure.[1] If the expulsion procedure complies with the above requirements, the courts will endorse the expulsion.[2]

1 With the possible exception of a two-man partnership, where the expulsion may be tantamount to a dissolution of the partnership.
2 *Carmichael v Evans* [1904] 1 Ch 486.

## INJUNCTIONS

**5.16** It has been noted in para 5.4 above that a partner owes duties to his co-partners, which are prescribed by case law, statute and provision in the partnership agreement. A partner may adopt a course of conduct either alone or in alliance with other partners, whereby he wilfully disregards the terms of the partnership agreement. A partner may also act in breach of any express or implied duty of good faith that he owes to his co-partner(s). This may be against the interests of a minority partner. In these circumstances the minority partner may seek an injunction to restrain the miscreant and destructive behaviour as an alternative to seeking the expulsion of the recalcitrant partner. An injunction, being an equitable remedy, will not be granted without sufficient or suitable cause.

**5.17** Accordingly, temporary or minor squabbles and disagreements between partners will not constitute sufficient or suitable grounds for the granting of equitable relief such as an injunction. However, a minority partner in a family partnership may seek an injunction so as to prevent the majority partner(s) from excluding him from involvement in the family business.[1] An injunction may also be sought by a minority partner so as to prevent the majority from using the assets of the partnership otherwise than in the course of the partnership enterprise.[2] It would appear from the authorities, that where the conduct which is the subject of a complaint is carried out by a partner who has been appointed as the managing partner by the partnership agreement, then an injunction restraining that partner's conduct will only be granted in the most exceptional circumstances.³

1 *Hall v Hall* (1855) 20 Beav 139.
2 Or to ensure the minority partner enjoys the benefit of the partnership assets. See also *Hawkins v Hawkins* (1858) 4 Jur NS 1044.
3 *Walker v Hirsch* (1884) 27 Ch D 460, CA.

**5.18** Since an injunction is an equitable remedy, a minority partner seeking this kind of relief must establish that he is not in breach of any obligations imposed upon him by case law, the Partnership Act 1890, or the partnership agreement. The minority partner must show that he is willing and able to perform the obligations imposed upon him by the partnership before he can seek to restrain any co-partner from any breach of his equivalent obligations. A minority partner's own misconduct may therefore, constitute a complete bar to a successful application for an injunction, irrespective of the conduct of the majority partner(s).¹

1 *Littlewood v Caldwell* (1822) 11 Price 97.

## APPOINTMENT OF A RECEIVER/MANAGER

**5.19** An injunction is not the only remedy available to a minority partner seeking to prevent a majority partner(s) from ignoring the obligations imposed upon them by the partnership, or being in breach of those obligations. The minority partner in a family partnership who is oppressed by the conduct of the majority, may apply to the court for the appointment of a receiver or manager to manage the affairs of the partnership. These remedies are draconian and should only be sought where there is no viable alternative, since the appointment of a receiver or manager affects all the members of the family partnership, including the minority partner who sought the appointment. The difference between a receiver and a manager has been set out by Lord Lindley:

> 'The object of having a receiver appointed by the court is to place the partnership assets under the protection of the court, and to prevent everybody, except the officer of the court, from in any way intermeddling with them. The object of having a manager is to have the partnership business carried on under the direction of the court, a receiver, unless he is also appointed manager, has no power to carry on the business.'¹

1 *Lindley* (17th edn) para 23.143.

**5.20** The courts are most reluctant to appoint a receiver without a subsequent dissolution of the partnership in mind.¹ Furthermore, the courts have never appointed a party as both a receiver and a manager unless a partnership was actually in the process of being dissolved. The courts may be willing to appoint a receiver to a family firm, without the need for the dissolution of the partnership in the following cases:

(a) Where the misconduct of the majority has produced a situation which places the partnership assets in jeopardy.² The courts will only make an appointment of a receiver under these circumstances where the misconduct of the majority is so serious as to destroy the mutual trust that must subsist between the members of the partnership.³

76   Minority protection

(b) Where the majority have wrongfully excluded the minority partner from involvement in the management of the partnership business, or prevented the minority partner from enjoying his interests in the partnership assets.[4]

1 For the nature of dissolution see Chapter 5, paras 5.22A and 5.23. For a fuller consideration of the concept see Prime & Scanlan *The Law of Partnership*, Chapter 12.
2 *Const v Harris* (1824) Turn & R 496.
3 Thus the remedy has been granted under the above ground where the miscreant partner has misappropriated partnership assets (*Sheppard v Oxenford* (1855) 1 K & J 491), and where the improper use of partnership assets and mismanagement of partnership affairs has endangered the whole enterprise (*Harding v Glover* (1810) 18 Ves 281).
4 *Doe d Warn v Horn* (1838) 3 M & W 333.

**5.21** In considering whether to appoint a receiver, the court will have regard to various matters. The larger the partnership the less likely the court will appoint a receiver, instead the court will usually be prepared to grant injunctive relief. Since the appointment of a receiver is a matter of discretion, the courts are reluctant to appoint a receiver where the family partnership is a professional practice, since an appointment may damage the standing of the firm.[1]

1 *Floydd v Cheney* [1970] Ch 602, [1970] 1 All ER 446.

CONCLUSION

**5.22** The remedy of seeking the appointment of a receiver is such a drastic remedy that it is rarely sought by a partner. Nevertheless the draconian nature of the remedy may be used as a bargaining chip by a minority partner in a family partnership to ensure a modification of the conduct of the majority of the partners in the firm.

DISSOLUTION

**5.22A** It may advisable to give a minority partner in a family partnership the right to seek the dissolution of the family partnership, either alone or as one of a prescribed number of partners. This will be a process whereby the firm ceases to carry on its business and is effectively brought to an end.[1] Provision may be made in the family partnership agreement for a partner to give notice to the other partners that the partnership is dissolved.[2]

1 A partnership may also be subject to a purely technical dissolution, for example on the death or retirement of a partner. In these cases the partnership continues in existence.
2 See 30 *Forms & Precedents* Form 1 (Formation checklist), para 20 and Form 2, clause 23.

DISSOLUTION BY COURT ORDER

**5.23** The grounds upon which a partnership may be dissolved by court order are also set out in ss 33–35 of the Partnership Act 1890. The statutory grounds which may be relevant for the purposes of a minority partner in a family partnership, and which could be used by such a partner who has been subject to oppressive conduct by the majority are:

(a) Conduct on the part of a partner, other than the partner seeking dissolution, which is calculated prejudicially to affect the running of the business of the partnership.[1] Under this ground, the court will consider the viewpoint of the partner seeking the dissolution as to whether the recalcitrant majority partner or partners has or have acted to the detriment of the partnership business. The court will be influenced by the size of the partnership and the fact that the partner or partners acting to the detriment of the partnership are the majority.[2]

(b) Dissolution on breach of the partnership agreement and destruction of mutual confidence.[3] This provision provides two separate grounds upon which a dissolution of a partnership may be sought by a minority partner. Either the majority partner or partners must wilfully or persistently be in breach of the partnership agreement, or the offending conduct of the majority must render the continuance of the partnership impractical.[4] In the latter circumstance, the mutual confidence that must subsist between partners must have been destroyed.[5]

(c) Dissolution on just and equitable grounds. This provision is a general purpose ground by which a court can order the dissolution of a partnership at the instigation of a minority partner. The provision is open-ended in its effect and is not restricted by the other provisions of the Partnership Act 1890 relating to dissolution and is construed by the courts sui generis. The courts are not prepared to interpret the provision so as to restrict its future application.[6] The courts will therefore dissolve a partnership under this provision if the objects of the partnership can no longer be achieved or at least achieved in the manner originally contemplated by the partners. Dissolution under this provision can only be sought by a minority partner if the other provisions of s 35 are inappropriate.[7]

1 Partnership Act 1890, s 35(c).
2 Conduct satisfying this ground should frequently constitute grounds for expulsion of the offending partner or partners. See 30 *Forms & Precedents* Form 2, clauses 22.1.1, 22.1.6 and 22.1.8.
3 Partnership Act 1890, s 35(d).
4 *Re Yenidje Tobacco Co Ltd* [1916] 2 Ch 426, CA.
5 Conduct by a partner which would justify the dissolution of the partnership under the above provision could also constitute grounds for expulsion of a partner. See 30 *Forms & Precedents* Form 2, clause 22.1.4, 22.1.8 and Form 92, clause 17.
6 *Ebrahimi v Westbourne Galleries Ltd* [1973] AC 360, [1972] 2 All ER 492, HL.
7 *Harrison v Tennant* (1856) 21 Beav 482.

**5.24** Dissolution of a partnership either by notice or court order is a drastic remedy. However, the threat brings the business of the family partnership to an end with the subsequent right of the minority partner to obtain his capital investment in the business,[1] and is an effective deterrent to an overbearing or oppressive majority partner or partnership.

1 And the right to prevent the majority partner(s) from commencing a new business under the old partnership name and thus reserving exclusively the goodwill of the firm. See 30 *Forms & Precedents* Form 2, clause 4 which vests the partnership name in the partners jointly.

## CONCLUSION

**5.25** The partnership is an ideal medium for the carrying on of a family business from the point of view of the family, member who holds a minority stake in the enterprise. The minority partner, both through the provisions of the Partnership Act and more particularly by recourse to provisions in a well drafted partnership agreement can ensure that his investment in the business is fully protected. Furthermore, the minority partner can ensure by these means that the majority cannot run the enterprise to the detriment of the minority. Superficially this is a marked improvement over the position of a minority shareholder in an incorporated family business. The problems for such an individual are now considered.

## THE MINORITY SHAREHOLDER IN THE FAMILY COMPANY

**5.26** A company registered under the Companies Act 1985 will recognise that the powers of the company are vested in two organs, these are prescribed in its constitution.[1] These organs are the directors of the company acting as a board, or the members of the company acting in a meeting. The minority shareholder must seek to protect his position within the constitution by ensuring that the company's affairs are not run solely in the interests of the majority shareholders to the detriment of the minority.

1 Through the memorandum and articles of association.

**5.27** A family private limited company differs in no way from any other private limited company. The minority shareholder in such a company may have recourse to certain remedies to protect his position, where the majority shareholders, who will also usually be the directors, conduct the affairs of the company to the detriment of the minority shareholder. In many cases the minority shareholder will not however, possess the financial resources to contest the actions of the majority through court action. In addition it may not be possible for him to obtain the necessary information on the affairs of the company to enable him to mount a successful challenge to the majority. Although the courts are ready to restrain the directors as a board or the majority of the members of a company from running the company in a manner which is clearly oppressive and prejudicial to the minority, they are unwilling to allow a minority shareholder or shareholders to obstruct the legitimate business interests of the directors and/or majority shareholders. The law therefore seeks to reconcile these competing and frequently conflicting interests.

## SPECIAL MAJORITIES

**5.28** Company law seeks to protect the position of the minority shareholder, by requiring that certain resolutions[1] may only be adopted by a company if a prescribed majority of members approve. Such resolutions may be either special or extraordinary resolutions.[2] However, a minority shareholder may not be able to muster sufficient votes to prevent the passing of either an extraordinary or special resolution by the majority even though the passing of a resolution would be detrimental to the interests of the minority shareholder. In these circumstances the minority shareholder must have recourse to other remedies.

1 By which a company authorises its officers to carry out company policy.
2 An extraordinary resolution is passed by a majority of not less than three quarters of members entitled to vote on the issue the subject of the resolution either in person, or where allowed,

by proxy, and where written notice specifying the intention to propose the resolution as an extraordinary resolution has been given, see the Companies Act 1985, s 378(1). A special resolution also requires the vote of the majority of members as in the case of an extraordinary resolution and where members must be given not less than 21 days notice of the intention to propose the resolution as a special resolution (s 378(2)). A resolution adopted by a bare majority at a meeting is an ordinary resolution.

## DIRECTOR'S DUTIES

**5.29** The directors of a family company owe certain duties to the company and more particularly to the shareholders in the company. The directors in exercising these duties must do so in good faith, and this includes having regard to the interests of the minority shareholder. Accordingly, the courts have been willing to protect or uphold the interests of the minority against the actions of the directors who will usually also constitute the majority shareholders in the company.

## ACTION AGAINST DIRECTORS

**5.30** The directors of the family company may have acted so as to be seen as having failed to take into account the best interests of the company.[1] For instance the disposal of some of the company's assets by the directors at an undervalue may damage the interests of both the minority shareholders and the company. In these circumstances the company has suffered an actionable wrong and could take legal action against the directors and any third parties involved in the disputed action. However, in the case of a family company the directors in the guise of the majority shareholders in a general meeting, or as the board of directors may ratify the disputed action.[2] In these cases it is therefore the majority shareholder/directors who determine whether the company will or will not initiate action against the directors.

1 Although what constitutes the company for these purposes remains unclear.
2 The directors of the company may be so empowered where the company's articles of association contain reg 70 of Table A. The directors may also disapply the rule against their profiting at the company's expense, or the rule against a conflict of interest arising between them and the company prior to taking the relevant action , see regs 84 and 85 of Table A. See Prime & Scanlan *The Law of Private Limited Companies*, Chapters 6 and 7.

**5.31** In these circumstances the courts recognise the right of a minority shareholder to institute proceedings on the company's behalf through a derivative action.[1] Such an action may be permitted as an exception to the so-called 'proper plaintiff' rule.[2] This rule reflects the policy of the courts not to entertain any action which involves matters or affairs of the company where the action is brought by a shareholder alone. The reasoning behind this policy is that the proper plaintiff in these cases is the company, which may decide not to institute proceedings through its constitutional organs. The situations where the courts will permit a shareholder to institute a derivative action are as follows.

1 So called because the action is derived from the company.
2 Formulated in the case of *Foss v Harbottle* (1843) 2 Hare 461, 67 ER 189.

## FRAUD ON THE MINORITY BY THOSE IN CONTROL

### The concept of control

**5.32** A minority shareholder may maintain a derivative action on the basis of fraud on the minority by those in control of the company. Although generally those in control of a family company will be the family members who are the directors/majority shareholders, this is not an absolute requirement. In *Prudential Assurance Co Ltd v Newman Industries Ltd (No 2)*[1] it was held that a derivative action could be maintained by a minority shareholder where the wrongdoers, although not holding the majority of shares[2] in the company, were able to manipulate their position in the company so as to ensure that the majority voted in accordance with their wishes in not allowing a claim to be brought by the company for the alleged wrong. De facto control is the key. It is suggested therefore that the shareholders in a family company who cast votes at a general meeting which ratifies, or which seeks to ratify the actions of the directors/shareholders of the company may therefore be disregarded, in so far as his or their interests conflict with those of the company. Within this context shareholders in a family company must consider the interests of the company as a whole when they exercise their voting power.[3]

1 [1981] Ch 257, [1980] 2 All ER 841; affd in this respect on appeal [1982] Ch 204, [1982] 1 All ER 354, CA.
2 Or being in a position to manipulate the board of directors.
3 *Ebrahimi v Westbourne Galleries Ltd* [1973] AC 360, [1972] 2 All ER 492, HL.

### FRAUD

**5.33** Fraud for the purposes of maintaining a derivative action would clearly include the director/majority shareholders appropriating company assets.[1] However, the concept of fraud is given a wide definition and application. Accordingly any activity by those in control of the company, usually the majority shareholders, which is intended or calculated to secure a benefit for the majority, at the expense of the minority, will constitute fraud for the purposes of maintaining a derivative action.[2]

1 *Menier v Hooper's Telegraph Works* (1874) 9 Ch App 350, CA.
2 *Cook v Deeks* [1916] 1 AC 554, PC.

**5.34** In the case of *Pavlides v Jensen*[1] the court refused to permit a derivative action against the directors of the company when the minority shareholder merely alleged that the directors had negligently sold company property at an undervalue. Nevertheless, fraud for the purposes of maintaining a derivative action, has been given a wide definition. In the case of *Daniels v Daniels*[2] a minority shareholder successfully forced a majority shareholder to account for profits made by the latter on the sale of company property to the majority shareholder at an undervalue. Although, as in the case of *Pavlides v Jensen*, no allegation of fraud was made, the case of *Daniels* was distinguished from *Pavlides* on the ground that the director in the latter case did not benefit from the relevant transaction.[3]

1 [1956] Ch 565, [1956] 2 All ER 518.
2 [1978] Ch 406, [1978] 2 All ER 89.
3 See also *Alexander v Automatic Telephone Co* [1900] 2 Ch 56, CA.

**5.35** In the case of *Clemens v Clemens Bros Ltd*[1] the court held that the issue of shares, or the exercise of voting rights can be fraudulent for the purposes of maintaining a derivative action if done by those in control of the company, or the majority shareholders, with the intention of harming the interests of the minority. In this case, there were two shareholders, one C and her niece. C held 55% of the shares and her niece 45%. Both of these shareholders had inherited their shares. The two could not agree on a common policy for the company. The niece therefore resigned her directorship. C exercised her voting rights in order to secure the passing of a resolution authorising the issue of new shares. The consequence of this action was the reduction of the niece's shareholding to less than 25% of the issued share capital of the company.[2] The court[3] held, in exercising its equitable jurisdiction, that it could permit the niece to maintain a derivative action so as to prevent C from using her legal right to exercise her majority voting power in any way she pleased.[4] The decision is barely reasoned in that the court justified its decision not on the application of any general principles, but on the ground that each case must be determined on its own facts. The court therefore could be regarded as having determined the case simply on the ground that it would have been inequitable to permit C to exercise her voting rights as majority shareholder subject to no restraint.[5]

1 [1976] 2 All ER 268.
2 With the consequence that C could secure the passing un-opposed of either extraordinary or special resolutions.
3 It should be noted that it was a first instance court.
4 In doing so the court approved *Ebrahimi v Westbourne Galleries Ltd* [1973] AC 360, [1972] 2 All ER 492, HL.
5 *Estmanco (Kilner House) Ltd v Greater London Council* [1982] 1 All ER 437, [1982] 1 WLR.

**5.36** Cases such as *Clemens* apply the case of *Ebrahimi v Westbourne Galleries Ltd*.[1] In that case Lord Wilberforce had first stated that the right of a shareholder to exercise his voting rights is subject to equitable considerations.[2] which may in certain circumstances render it unjust for a shareholder to exercise his voting rights in a given way. This is an amorphous concept and it is difficult to predict how it will be applied in any particular case.[3] In addition, since equity requires those who seek its aid to have 'clean hands', the courts may refuse relief to a minority shareholder in a family company, despite the actions of the majority, if the court considers that the minority shareholder has himself acted improperly.

1 [1973] AC 360, [1972] 2 All ER 492, HL.
2 Though this principle must be reconciled with the authorities which determine that a shareholder owes no duty to his co-shareholders when he exercises his voting rights in a company meeting. See Jessel MR in *Pender v Lushington* (1877) 6 Ch D 70. In these cases shareholders are in a different position from co-partners.
3 Despite the rationalisation of the above authorities and the attempt to lay down general principles of when a derivative action may be maintained by a minority shareholder by Vinelott J in the case of *Prudential Assurance Co Ltd v Newman Industries Ltd (No 2)* [1980] 2 All ER 841 at 869.

## COMPANIES ACT 1985, s 459

**5.37** Although it has been suggested that the derivative action may be maintained by a minority shareholder on the basis that his individual rights as a shareholder have been infringed,[1] this principle has not been universally accepted.[2] The difficulties in maintaining a derivative action have resulted in a number of statutory remedies being available to the minority shareholder who finds his position jeopardised by the actions of the majority.

1 *Re a Company (No 005136 of 1986)* [1987] BCLC 82.
2 The derivative action has been maintained on other grounds which were espoused in *Edwards v Halliwell* [1950] 2 All ER 1064 at 1067, CA which have not been set out in the text since they do not depend on the oppression of the minority shareholder per se for their application.

**5.38** By s 459(1) of the Companies Act 1985, a shareholder in a company, including a family company, may apply to the court by petition for an order under ss 459 and 461 of the Act. The grounds for any such order are that the company's affairs are being, or have been conducted in a manner which is unfairly prejudicial to the interests of its shareholders generally or to some of its shareholders, including a minority shareholder in a family company, or that any actual or proposed act or omission on its behalf would be so prejudicial.

**5.39** This remedy is most appropriate for the minority shareholder who is a member of what may be described as a quasi-partnership company. Such companies are little more than partnerships which have been incorporated by its members. The family company is a prime example of such a company. The judiciary have not however always been the most enthusiastic supporters of this remedy. In the case of *Re Unisoft Group Ltd (No 3)*[1] Harman J expressed the following opinion:[2]

> 'Petitions under s 459 have become notorious to the judges of this court – and I think also to the bar – for their length, their unpredictability of management, and the enormous and appalling costs which are incurred upon them particularly by reason of the volume of documents to be produced.'

1 [1994] 1 BCLC 609.
2 At 611.

**5.40** Despite these criticisms minority shareholders often have recourse to a petition under s 459 even though it is a costly remedy.

ORDERS UNDER A PETITION

**5.41** Section 461(2) sets out the orders a court may make following a petition made under s 459(1). These orders are set out below in outline:

(a) The court may by order regulate the conduct of the company's affairs. This would include altering the company's memorandum and/or articles of association, in appropriate circumstances.
(b) The court may by order require the company to refrain from carrying out any act or continuing to do any such act which is the subject of the complaint by the petitioner.
(c) The court may by order give authority for proceedings to be brought in the name of the company by any person as the court may direct.[1]
(d) The court may by order make provision for the purchase of the shares of any of the shareholders of the company by any other shareholder or by the company itself.[2]

1 The court may thus authorise the bringing of a derivative action under s 459.
2 This will be the most appropriate remedy or order where the relationship between the members of the family company have broken down, with or without fault, but the business cannot

continue unless one of the family members leaves the business. In these cases the members of the family who are crucial to the survival of the family company may under a petition be ordered to purchase the shares of a petitioner. See *Re A Company* [1986] BCLC 362; *Re A Company (No 004377 of 1986)* [1987] 1 WLR 102. For the problems of valuation of shares see Prime & Scanlan *The Law of Private Limited Companies*, Chapter 15; Prime, Gale and Scanlan *The Law and Practice of Joint Ventures*, Chapters 4 and 5.

**5.42** The last order is the most commonly made. One of the greatest disadvantages for a minority shareholder in a family company is the difficulty in realising his investment in the business should he become involved in an acrimonious dispute with the majority, or where he is the victim of oppressive conduct instituted by the latter. The minority shareholder is at a disadvantage when compared to a minority partner in a family partnership. The order noted in (d) above may place the minority shareholder in a similar position to his counterpart in a family partnership.

**5.43** The powers which a court has under ss 459 and 461 are discretionary. Nevertheless, unlike a derivative action which may be subject to equitable principles it is not necessary that the petitioner has acted fairly and honestly with regard to the company's affairs for the petition to be successful. Thus a petition will not be struck out on the ground that the behaviour of the petitioner is questionable.[1] However, the conduct of the petitioner may be relevant in the decision of the court as to whether relief will be granted under s 461, or the nature of the relief which is so ordered.

1 *Re London School of Electronics Ltd* [1986] Ch 211.

**5.44** It would appear that many petitions under s 459 are sought, but it seems that few reach full trial. Many of the cases on s 459 which are reported have been determined on preliminary issues. This would suggest that a petition frequently results in a negotiated settlement, a testament to the effectiveness of the provision. In these circumstances the prohibitive costs of an action under s 459 noted by Harman J may prove an incentive to encourage the resolution of disputes between shareholders.

MEANING OF INTEREST

**5.45** It is clear from the authorities that the conduct that is the subject of a petition must be unfairly prejudicial to the interests of the petitioner as a shareholder.[1] Section 459 refers to a shareholder's interests. The company's memorandum and articles of association will prescribe the shareholder's rights. The concept of interests is wider than rights. In the case of *Re a Company*,[2] Hoffmann J, relying upon the equitable doctrine espoused by Lord Wilberforce in *Ebrahimi v Westbourne Galleries Ltd*,[3] decided that the word 'unfairly' within s 459 allowed the court to have recourse to equitable considerations in determining the nature of a shareholder's interests for the purposes of an action under s 459.[4] Hoffmann J, in applying these equitable considerations, determined that the court could recognise that the rights and expectations of shareholders for the purposes of s 459 were wider than any rights that may be prescribed in the company's memorandum and articles of association. In the case, a shareholder who had ventured capital to the enterprise on the understanding with the other shareholders that he would participate in the management of the company, and had a reasonable expectation that he would continue in his role as a director of the company. Accordingly his removal from the board was to be regarded as being unfairly prejudicial to him and to his interests as a shareholder, within the terms of s 459. The case gives a very wide interpretation of 'interests', which increases the usefulness of s 459 as a remedy for a minority shareholder within the family company. Nevertheless, it is difficult to reconcile this wide interpretation of 'interests' with authorities which have defined the nature of a shareholder's rights as prescribed in the company's constitutional documents.[5]

1 *Re JE Cade & Son Ltd* [1992] BCLC 213.
2 [1986] BCLC 376.
3 [1973] AC 360, [1972] 2 All ER 492, HL.
4 Hoffmann J thus rejected the reasoning of Lord Grantchester in *Re a Company (No 004475 of 1982)* [1983] Ch 178, [1983] 2 All ER 36. However, Hoffmann J's approach has been followed see *Potgate & Denby (Agencies) Ltd* [1987] BCLC 8; *Re Blue Arrow plc* [1987] BCLC 585.
5 See *Beattie v E & F Beattie Ltd* [1938] Ch 708, [1938] 3 All ER 214, CA which determined that provisions in the articles of association can only bind a shareholder in his capacity as a shareholder and not in another capacity such as a director of the company. See also the case of *Eley v Positive Government Security Life Assurance Co Ltd* (1876) 1 Ex D 88, CA, where the court held that the right of a shareholder to hold the position as permanent legal adviser to the company as prescribed in the articles of association was not a right enforceable by the plaintiff in his capacity as a shareholder. The only way to reconcile these cases with the views of Hoffmann J is by accepting that the family company as a species of incorporated partnership is subject to its own legal regime.

## UNFAIRLY PREJUDICIAL

**5.46** The requirement that the company's affairs must have been conducted in a manner which is unfairly prejudicial to the interests of the petitioner as a shareholder in the company has been interpreted widely by the courts. In the case of *Re a Company (008699 of 1985)*[1] the court held that the term 'unfairly prejudicial' was intended to confer an unfettered jurisdiction upon the courts hearing any applications under s 459. The court was unwilling to restrict its jurisdiction by adding any gloss to the plain and ordinary meaning of the term.

1 [1986] BCLC 382 at 388.

**5.47** However, the courts have been prepared to hold that where the conduct which is the subject of a petition constitutes no more than poor management and which causes a shareholder to suffer consequential damage to his interests then this is not unfairly prejudicial to a minority shareholder's interests. A petitioner under the section has no right, even in the case of a family company, to expect a reasonable standard of management of the company.[1]

1 In the case of *Re Elgindata* [1991] BCLC 959 Warner J thus expressed the opinion that at 994:

'Where the majority shareholders, for reasons of their own, persisted in retaining in charge of the management of the company's business a member of their family who was demonstrably incompetent.'

There was no unfair prejudice to a shareholder's interests. Despite the above it would appear that 'unfairly prejudicial' as a concept will not cover an unlimited or undefined number of situations see *Scottish Co-operative Wholesale Society Ltd v Meyer* [1959] AC 324, [1958] 3 All ER 66, HL.

**5.48** The majority shareholders/directors of the family company may however, as an aspect of poor management of the business withhold the payment of dividends. This will frequently be combined with the approval of large fees for the directors. The accumulation of capital that may result from non-payment of dividends will generally be of disproportionate benefit to the majority shareholders. Such conduct can clearly be shown to be unfairly prejudicial to the interests of the minority.[1]

1 *Re Sam Weller & Sons Ltd* [1990] Ch 682; *Re Cumana Ltd* [1986] BCLC 430, CA. For the orders that are appropriate in such cases under s 461 see *Re a Company (No 004415 of 1996)* [1997] 1 BCLC 479.

## RE HARMER LTD

**5.49** The case of *Re HR Harmer Ltd*[1] is an instructive case on the application of s 459 to the family company.[2] H had formed a private limited company to take over his business. The business prospered and in time the bulk of the shares were held by the sons of H. However, H retained effective control of the company. He was appointed 'governing director by the articles of association of the company'[3] and his sons were appointed directors. According to the sons, who were the petitioners, the father ran the company in a dictatorial manner, blithely ignoring his co-directors and any resolutions of the board of directors and the interests of the shareholders. H ran the company as if it were still his business. H founded an unprofitable overseas branch of the business without consulting his co-directors. He would also, for instance, claim unauthorised expenses for himself and his wife. He was also alleged to have behaved in an unpleasant and bullying manner towards staff. Finally H sought to sell off a profitable part of the business which would have damaged the goodwill of the company.

1 [1958] 3 All ER 689, [1959] 1 WLR 62, CA.
2 The case concerned the statutory precursor to s 459, which for the purposes of the text was in the same form as s 459.
3 Although this position was not invested with any special or distinctive powers.

**5.50** Roxburgh J granted the sons the relief they sought. In addition he ordered the following:

(a) That the company should employ H as a 'consultant', at a named salary under a contract for services;
(b) That H should not interfere in the company's affairs, otherwise than in accordance with a valid decision of the board of directors;
(c) That H should be appointed president of the company for life, but that this office should not impose on H any duties, rights or powers.

On appeal the order of Roxburgh J was upheld.

## JUST AND EQUITABLE GROUND FOR WINDING UP A COMPANY UNDER THE INSOLVENCY ACT 1986, s 122(1)(g)

**5.51** This remedy is drastic and draconian within the context of the family company. The courts are unwilling to define or limit the grounds upon which they will exercise their jurisdiction to wind up a company under this provision.[1]

The leading case on this provision is *Ebrahimi v Westbourne Galleries Ltd*.[2] Two of three director/shareholders of a company exercised their rights to dismiss the third director/shareholder. In so doing they observed the strict legal formalities.[3] The two remaining directors subsequently ensured that no dividends were paid, so that in effect the removed director was prevented from receiving any return on his investment in the company. He sought to have the company wound up under the immediate statutory precursor of s 122(1)(g).[4] Lord Wilberforce held that the words 'just and equitable' within the statutory context permitted the court to recognise the rights, expectations and obligations of the shareholders inter se, and to wind up a company if these matters were being thwarted.[5] In this regard the court could wind up a company notwithstanding that there had been no misconduct on the part of the members of the company or the directors, it will be sufficient that the parties are in deadlock.[6] The provision will apply particularly to the family company which is similar to a partnership. The court was prepared to give consideration and to refer to the just and equitable grounds which will be relevant to winding up a partnership under the Partnership Act 1890.[7] in determining whether to wind up a company. Perhaps one of the most common grounds justifying the winding up of a family company under s 122(1)(g) is the dictatorial or unreasonable behaviour of a director, or those in control of the company.[8]

1 For the equivalent ground in partnerships see para 5.23 above and Prime & Scanlan T*he Law of Partnership*, p 270.
2 [1973] AC 360, [1972] 2 All ER 492, HL although the case concerned the statutory precursor of s 122(1)(g), which was identical in form.
3 Section 303 of the Companies Act 1985 currently allows the removal of a director following the passing of an ordinary resolution to that effect.
4 Which was similar in form.
5 See *Re Yenidje Tobacco Co Ltd* [1916] 2 Ch 426, CA; *Re A and BC Chewing Gum Ltd* [1975] 1 All ER 1017, [1975] 1 WLR 579.
6 As was the case in *Re Yenidje Tobacco Co Ltd* (ibid)
7 See para 5.23 above.
8 *Loch v John Blackwood Ltd* [1924] AC 783, PC.

CONCLUSION

**5.52** The remedies considered in this chapter which seek to prevent the minority shareholder in the family company from oppression are either less flexible than the equivalent remedies available to a minority partner in a family partnership, or more expensive and time consuming. In particular, the jurisdiction of the courts both under ss 459 and 122(1)(g) is based on the proposition that the memorandum and articles of association do not contain all the arrangements between the parties regulating their rights and obligations. Accordingly, to seek to protect the interests of the minority shareholder solely on the basis of the constitutional documents may be to defeat the legitimate expectations of the shareholders.[1] The legal profession has sought to give full effect to the supposed intentions of the parties in this regard, not by the continued adaptation of the constitutional documents, which are public documents requiring registration, but by recourse to the shareholder agreement.

1 *Re a Company* [1985] BCLC 80.

## THE SHAREHOLDER AGREEMENT

**5.53** The shareholder agreement may be used by the shareholders in a family company so as to bring about a partnership relationship between the parties although within the structure of a private limited company. The effectiveness of these agreements was recognised in the case of *Russell v Northern Bank Development Corpn Ltd*.[1] The provisions in a shareholder agreement may be similar to equivalent provisions in a partnership agreement. The shareholder agreement constitutes a contract between the shareholders, and also between the company and the shareholders, provided that the company does not undertake any responsibility or commitment which it could not lawfully promise.

1 [1992] 3 All ER 161, [1992] 1 WLR 588, HL. See also the article by Brian Davenport QC (1993) 109 LQR 553.

**5.54** A shareholder agreement therefore may make provision so as to prevent the shareholders in a family company from passing any resolutions without unanimity. The shareholder agreement may give a minority shareholder a power to veto the exercise of powers that could otherwise be exercised by the majority shareholders in a company. The shareholder agreement may therefore effectively protect the minority shareholder from the oppressive conduct of the majority. In the event of a dispute between the parties to the agreement, the first point of reference will be the shareholder agreement and not the memorandum and articles of association of the company. The use of the shareholder agreement by the shareholders in a family company may therefore render the protection of the minority shareholder from oppression by the majority in practical terms little different from the protection of the minority partner in a family partnership through recourse to the provisions in the partnership agreement.[1]

1 See above for a consideration of the ways in which a minority partner may protect himself from oppressive conduct by recourse to provisions in the partnership agreement.

# Chapter 6

# Winding up and insolvency of family businesses

**6.1** The family business in either its incorporated or unincorporated form bears the risk that it may fail financially bringing potential ruin to its members. It is received wisdom that the incorporation of the family business means that should the enterprise fail then the liability of the members is limited to the value of the shares held in the enterprise. By way of contrast, the insolvency of the family partnership will render the separate estates of each of the members liable to account in full for the debts of the business, bringing possible bankruptcy to the members and penury to their respective families. This chapter will consider the reality behind these assumptions.[1] This chapter will also outline the various procedures whereby a family business may be wound up or dissolved as a consequence of being insolvent. The insolvency procedures applicable to a partnership will be considered first.

1 These are based on sound legal provisions, see *Saloman v A Saloman & Co Ltd* [1897] AC 22, HL.

## THE INSOLVENT PARTNERSHIP – INSOLVENCY PROCEDURES

**6.2** The family partnership like any other partnership may be dissolved on the grounds of insolvency. In outline the procedures[1] for winding up an insolvent partnership are as follows.

1 The text will concentrate on the procedures likely to be applicable to family partnerships.

## WINDING UP OF PARTNERSHIP AS UNREGISTERED COMPANY

**6.3** A family partnership may be wound up as if it were an unregistered company. In these circumstances the Insolvency Act 1986, Pt V, ss 220–229, which govern the winding up of an unregistered company, apply to partnerships by virtue of the Insolvent Partnerships Order 1994.[1] A partnership subject to these provisions may be wound up either with or without concurrent bankruptcy[2] petitions being presented against the partners.

1 SI 1994/2421, as amended by SI 1996/1308, art 2.
2 The text assumes the partners in a family partnership will be private individuals and not companies.

## WINDING UP OF INSOLVENT PARTNERSHIP WITHOUT CONCURRENT PETITION

**6.4** The grounds for winding up an insolvent partnership as an unregistered company without concurrent petitions are:

(a) That the partnership is dissolved, or has ceased to carry on business or is carrying on business only for the purposes of winding up its affairs.

(b) Where the partnership is unable to pay its debts.[1] This may arise where the liabilities of the partnership, exceed the value of the partnership assets.

(c) Where the court is of the opinion that it is just and equitable that the partnership be wound up.

1 See s 221(7) of the Insolvency Act 1986 as applied and modified by the Insolvent Partnerships Order 1994, SI 1994/2421, Sch 3, art 7. This provision sets out prescribed situations where a partnership will be regarded as being unable to pay its debts. Space does not permit a consideration of these provisions, see 30 *Forms & Precedents*, para 178. The principal situation is where a creditor serves a written demand on the partnership for a sum exceeding £750 which is owed to him by the partnership, and the sum has neither been paid, secured nor compounded within three weeks of serving the demand.

## PARTIES WHO MAY PRESENT PETITION

**6.5** The principal parties who may present a petition under the above provisions are the creditors of the partnership. This will include a contingent or prospective creditor or a creditor by assignment.[1] A partner may present a petition where the partnership consists of not less than eight partners.[2]

1 Other parties are prescribed under s 221A(1) of the Insolvency Act 1986 as applied and inserted by the Insolvent Partnerships Order 1994, SI 1994/2421 as amended by SI 1996/1308, art 2. These parties include the trustees of a present or former partner's estate, the administrator of the partnership, the supervisor of a voluntary arrangement under Pt VIII of the 1986 Act. Other parties have not been referred to in the text since they are not likely to present petitions against the normal family partnership.
2 Insolvency Act 1986, s 221A(1).

## CONSEQUENCES OF PRESENTATION OF PETITION

**6.6** The winding up of an insolvent partnership as an unregistered company is deemed to commence on the presentation of the petition.[1] From that moment on no disposition of partnership assets or a change in the membership of the partnership has any legal effect unless approved by the court.[2]

1 Insolvency Act 1986, s 129(2).
2 Ibid.

## WINDING UP ORDER AGAINST INSOLVENT PARTNERSHIP WITH CONCURRENT PETITION(S)

**6.7** A family partnership may be wound up as an unregistered company with concurrent petitions against a member or members of the partnership.[1] If a creditor petitions for the winding up of the insolvent partnership while seeking a concurrent petition, then a minimum of one partner needs to be the subject of such a petition concurrently with the partnership.[2] The sole ground upon which an insolvent partnership may be wound up where a concurrent petition is presented is that the partnership is unable to pay its debts.[3]

1 Including former partners, see the Insolvent Partnerships Order 1994, SI 1994/2421 Sch 3, arts 8, 10, Schs 4 , 6.
2 Insolvent Partnerships Order 1994, SI 1994/2421, art 8(1).
3 For this ground see above. See s 221(8) and s 221(1) of the Insolvency Act 1986 as modified by the Insolvent Partnerships Order 1994, SI 1994/2421 Schs 4 and 6.

**6.8** A partner may also present a winding up petition against the partnership together with a concurrent bankruptcy petition or petitions against his co-partner(s) on the ground that the partnership is unable to pay its debts. Concurrent bankruptcy petitions must be presented by the petitioning partner against the partnership, and all the other partners, including himself or itself, all of whom must be willing to have insolvency orders made against them.[1]

1 Section 124(2) as modified by the Insolvent Partnerships Order 1994, Sch 6, art 10.

## JOINT PETITION BY ALL THE PARTNERS TO WIND UP THE PARTNERSHIP

**6.9** This insolvency procedure involves all of the partners presenting a joint debtor's petition against the partnership but the partnership is not wound up as an unregistered company. This procedure is appropriate for family partnerships since all of the partners must be private individuals and they must all agree to this action. The only ground for the presentation of a petition in the above circumstances is that the partnership is unable to pay its debts.[1]

1 Section 264 and s 272(1) of the Insolvency Act 1986 as modified by the Insolvent Partnerships Order 1994, Sch 7, art 11.

## PETITION FOR BANKRUPTCY PRESENTED AGAINST ONE OR MORE PARTNERS BUT WITH NO ATTEMPT TO WIND UP THE PARTNERSHIP

**6.10** Where a partnership debt remains unpaid, a creditor has an option of presenting a petition for bankruptcy against one, but not necessarily all the partners, without seeking to have the partnership wound up as an unregistered company.[1] Regard must be had to the possible application of art 14(2) of the Insolvent Partnerships Order to such proceedings. Where a bankruptcy petition has been presented to the court against a partner, and the court is made aware that the partner is a member of an insolvent partnership, the court may apply the provisions of the Insolvent Partnerships Order to these proceedings, and make any order with any necessary modifications.[2]

1 The proceedings will therefore be governed by the provisions of the Insolvency Act 1986.
2 Sections 303(2A)–(2C) as inserted by the Insolvent Partnerships Order 1994, art 14(2).

## THE POSITION OF PARTNERS IN THE WINDING UP OF THE PARTNERSHIP

**6.11** Where a family partnership is wound up as an unregistered company each of the partners will be regarded in two capacities:

(a) as a contributory, that is a person liable to contribute to the assets of the partnership in the event of a winding up;[1] and
(b) as an officer of the partnership.[2]

A contributory will include any person held out as a partner, any outgoing partner who remains directly liable to the creditors of the partnership or, an outgoing partner who has agreed to bear a proportion of a particular ongoing liability which continues to be incurred by his former partners.

1 Insolvency Act 1986, s 226.
2 Insolvency Act 1986 as modified by the Insolvent Partnerships Order 1994, Sch 4. See also s 221(7). This renders the partners subject to certain provisions of the Insolvency Act 1986 and the Company Directors (Disqualification) Act 1986. The nature of these provisions will be considered at para 6.88 below in the context of corporate insolvency.

## THE PARTNER AS CONTRIBUTOR

**6.12** The liability of a contributory partner is unlimited. However, there may be adjustments to any contribution made by that partner as between the various members of the partnership in order to ensure that any contribution made by a partner reflects the terms of the partnership agreement, and the agreed ratio of the sharing of the profits and losses of the business between the members of the partnership.[1] Former partners will be held liable to contribute to the settlement of debts incurred by the partnership whilst they were partners.

1 Insolvency Act 1986, s 226(1) and (2).

**6.13** The person appointed as the liquidator of the partnership draws up the list of the contributories and subsequently may make calls upon them to settle the partnership's debts and liabilities.[1] The liquidator is also responsible for the adjustment of contributions between the contributing partners.[2] Enforcement of any payment required by a call is by order of the court.[3]

1 Insolvency Act 1986, s 160(b) and (d); Insolvency Rules 1986, rr 4.195 and 4.202; Insolvency Act 1986, s 148, Insolvency Rules 1986, rr 4.196–198, s 150.
2 Insolvency Act 1986, s 154; Insolvency Rules 1986, rr 4.221–222.
3 Ibid s 228, r 4.205(2).

**6.14** Once a winding up order against a partnership as an unregistered company is made then the authority of all the partners to bind the partnership is revoked. All partners are under an obligation to deliver to the liquidator any partnership assets in their possession.[1] Partners may be required to submit a statement which may inter alia contain details of the partnership's assets, debts and liabilities.[2] The purpose of these provisions is to establish the assets and liabilities of the partner's separate estates, since it is only the partnership assets which vest in the liquidator.

1 Partnership Act 1890, s 20; Insolvency Act 1986, s 234 as modified by art 7 of and Sch 3 to the 1994 Order.
2 Insolvency Act 1986, s 131(1) as modified by art 7 of and Sch 3 to the 1994 Order.

## ADMINISTRATION OF PARTNERS AND PARTNERSHIP ESTATES

**6.15** The application of insolvency legislation to partnerships recognises the separation of the partnership debts and liabilities, the joint estate, and the separate estates and debts of the individual partners. It is the primary principle of insolvency law and practice with regard to partnerships, that the joint creditors should first be paid out of the partnership assets, that is the joint estate, and that the separate creditors of each partner should first be paid out of the separate estate of each partner. If, after satisfying all the claims of the joint creditors, there is a surplus, such sums can be used to satisfy the claims of the creditors of the respective separate estates in so far as any claims remain unsatisfied and vice versa.[1] These principles are set out in detail in the Schedules to the Insolvent Partnerships Order 1994.

1 *Re Rudd & Son Ltd* [1984] Ch 237, [1984] 3 All ER 225.

## EXPENSES INCURRED BY RESPONSIBLE INSOLVENCY PRACTITIONER

**6.16** The joint estate shall first be applied in payment of the joint expenses incurred by the liquidator in winding up the insolvent partnership. The separate estate of each insolvent partner is applicable in the first instance in payment of the separate expenses in the bankruptcy of the relevant partner.

**6.17** Where the joint estate is insufficient for the above purposes, then the unpaid balance will be apportioned equally between the separate estates of the insolvent members of the partnership against whom insolvency orders have been made, and will form part of the expenses to be paid out of those estates.

## PRIORITY OF DEBTS IN JOINT ESTATE

**6.18** After payment of expenses,[1] the joint debts of the partnership are to be paid out of the joint estate in the following order of priority:

(a) preferential debts,[2]
(b) debts which are neither preferential nor postponed,[3]
(c) interest under s 189 of the Insolvency Act 1986 on the joint debts, other than postponed debts,[4]
(d) postponed debts,
(e) interest under s 189 of the Insolvency Act 1986 on the postponed debts.

1 Section 175, s 175C and s 328, 328A of the Insolvency Act 1986.
2 These include national insurance payments.
3 Such debts are the ordinary partnership debts.
4 Such debts include sums owed by the partnership to an individual partner. See also s 3 of the Partnership Act 1890.

**6.19** The liquidator should adjust the rights of the members of the partnership as contributories and distribute any surplus to the partners, or where applicable, to the separate estates of the members, according to their respective rights and interests in it.

**6.20** Both the preferential debts and the debts which are neither preferential nor postponed, and which are known as the joint debts, rank equally between themselves. If the joint estate is insufficient to meet these debts, they abate in equal proportions between themselves.

**6.21** Where the joint estate is not sufficient for the payment of the joint debts, then the liquidator should aggregate the value of those debts to the extent that they have not been satisfied, or are not capable of being satisfied, and that aggregate amount shall be a claim against the separate estate of each member of the partnership against whom an insolvency order has been made which:

(a) is a debt provable by the liquidator in each such estate; and
(b) should rank equally with the debts of the partners referred to in s 175B(1)(b) and s 328B(1)(b) of the Insolvency Act 1986, that is the non-preferential and non-postponed debts.

**6.22** Where the liquidator receives any distribution from the separate estate of a partner in respect of any of the joint debts and liabilities, such sums become part of the joint estate and will be distributed in accordance with the order of priority noted above.

PRIORITY OF DEBTS IN SEPARATE ESTATES

**6.23** The order of priority of debts in respect of the separate estate of a partner is as follows:

The separate estate of each member of the partners against whom the insolvency order has been made shall be applied, after payment of expenses, in accordance with ss 175 and 328 of the Insolvency Act 1986 and subject to ss 175C(2) and 328C(2) in payment of the separate debts of the partner in an order of priority which mirrors that for the joint estate noted above. The debts in each class of debts rank equally. Where the separate estate is insufficient to meet any particular class of debts, they abate in equal proportions between themselves.

**6.24** Any distributions received from the joint estate, or from the separate estate of any other partner against whom an insolvency order has been made, become part of the relevant separate estate and are distributed in accordance with the order of priority noted above.

PRIORITY OF DEBTS

**6.25** Consideration has already been given to the principle that the joint estate and debts and the separate estates and debts are dealt with in insolvency proceedings in accordance with strict rules of priority. Joint debts are first satisfied out of the joint estate. All debts rank equally, except for preferential debts.[1] Debts under s 3 of the Partnership Act 1890 are postponed.[2] Any surplus assets of the joint estate may be used to satisfy the separate creditors of the individual partners. The separate estates of each individual partner must first satisfy the creditors of that individual partner. Any balance may then be used to satisfy the joint creditors. There can be no transfer of assets between the separate estates of the partners to satisfy the unmet liabilities of an individual partner.

1 Insolvency Act 1986, s 386 and Sch 6 which lists such debts.
2 By s 2(3)(d) of the Partnership Act 1890, a party may lend money to the partnership and receive a varying rate of interest dependent on the profits, or receive a share of the profits arising from the carrying on of the business without that party becoming a partner. This is dependent on the loan contract being in writing. However, s 3 of the Act provides that the right of that party to recover the loan is postponed in the case of the insolvency of the partnership until the claims of the other creditors have been satisfied.

## Conclusion

**6.26** Although the partnership is an unincorporated business entity and the partners are liable for the debts of the partnership to the full extent of their estates, the insolvency procedures applicable to partnerships recognise that the estates of the partners are distinct from that of the partnership. The liquidator must first seek to satisfy the debts of the business from the partnership assets under the procedure for the winding up of a partnership as an unregistered company with concurrent bankruptcy petitions. The insolvent family partnership, therefore, bears some similarities to the insolvent family company.[1] The Insolvent Partnerships Order has further reduced the distinction between the family company and the family partnership by making it possible for a partnership as well as a company to enter into a voluntary arrangement with its creditors.[2] The order applies Pt I of the Insolvency Act 1986, (which concerns company voluntary arrangements), to insolvent partnerships, with suitable modifications. An insolvent family partnership as an entity may, therefore, conclude a legally effective arrangement with its creditors. By such an arrangement it may discharge its debts and return itself to financial health, without resort by either the partners or the partnership creditors to the drastic insolvency procedures that have been considered in para 6.3 above. The application of this procedure to the family partnership has made the partnership an even more flexible business enterprise and is a further indication of how the partnership in effect takes on some aspects of a corporate business vehicle.

1 See para 6.68 below.
2 Insolvent Partnerships Order 1994, art 4 and Sch 1.

## VOLUNTARY ARRANGEMENTS

**6.27** The partners in an insolvent family partnership may propose a voluntary arrangement, but not if the partnership is subject to an administration order,[1] or is being wound up as an unregistered company, or where an order for the winding up of the partnership has been made on the joint bankruptcy petition of the partners. However, in the above circumstances, the administrator, the liquidator or the trustee in bankruptcy may themselves propose such an arrangement.

1 See para 6.30 below for a consideration of the nature of an administration order.

**6.28** The proposal will usually take the form of a composition with the partnership's creditors in satisfaction of the debts of the partnership, or a scheme of arrangement of its affairs.[1] The proposal must provide a nominee, who must be a qualified insolvency practitioner, to act as trustee of the voluntary arrangement and to supervise its operation.[2]

1 Insolvency Act 1986, s 1, as modified by Sch 1 to the 1994 Order.
2 Ibid.

**6.29** One of the procedures that the insolvency practitioner must follow is to report to the court on matters such as whether the arrangement should be preceded with. Following this, the practitioner should summon a meeting of the creditors.[1] That meeting determines whether the arrangement should be approved with or without modifications. If the meeting approves the arrangement, it will then bind all the creditors of the partnership, and the court may stay any insolvency proceedings against the insolvent partnership, or discharge any administration order. The court may give directions to facilitate the implementation of the arrangement.[2]

1 Insolvency Act 1986, s 3, as modified.
2 Ibid s 5, as modified.

## ADMINISTRATION ORDERS

**6.30** Administration orders can apply to insolvent partnerships, though in a modified form, by virtue of the Insolvent Partnerships Order 1994.[1]

1 Article 6 of and Sch 2 to the 1994 Order.

**6.31** Where the court is satisfied that a partnership is unable to pay its debts,[1] the court may make an administration order in relation to a partnership. The court will appoint an administrator who must be a qualified insolvency practitioner. The purposes of such an order are as follows:

(a) to secure the survival of the partnership as a whole or in part as a going concern;
(b) to secure the approval of a voluntary arrangement;[2]
(c) to secure a more advantageous realisation of the partnership property than would be affected by a winding up.

1 See para 6.4, n 1 above for a consideration of this concept.
2 As noted in para 6.28 above.

**6.32** An administration order cannot be made in respect of a partnership which is already the subject of a winding up order as an unregistered company, or where the partnership has been wound up on the joint bankruptcy petition of the partners, without the partnership being wound up as an unregistered company.[1]

1 Insolvency Act 1986, as modified by Sch 2 to the 1994 Order.

**6.33** The purpose of an administration order is therefore to rehabilitate the partnership as a going concern, or at least to secure a more advantageous realisation of the partnership assets if it is subsequently wound up, and thus to preserve the separate estates of the partners as a whole or in part.

**6.34** The effect of making an application for an administration order is to impose a moratorium on the affairs of the partnership from the date of application to the date when the court either makes the order or dismisses the application. The partnership, therefore, cannot be wound up. In addition, any further insolvency proceedings are rendered inapplicable.[1]

1 Insolvency Act 1986, ss 10 and 11, as modified.

**6.35** All persons dealing with a partnership during the subsistence of an administration order must be notified of this fact. All partnership documents must therefore give notice of the fact.[1]

1 Insolvency Act 1986, s 12, as modified.

**6.36** The powers of the administrator of an insolvent partnership are the same as those of the partners whom the administrator supplants. The administrator may therefore do all things that are necessary for the management of the affairs of the partnership and of the partnership property.[1]

1 Insolvency Act 1986, s 13, as modified.

CONCLUSION

**6.37** The administration order is a flexible mechanism which may permit a failing family partnership to be nursed back to financial health under the guidance of a court-appointed insolvency practitioner. The personal bankruptcy of the partners may therefore be avoided. The recent application of this procedure to the partnership is yet another example of the narrowing of the distinction between the family partnership and the family company. Consideration should now be given to the various forms of insolvency procedure that may be available in the case of the private limited company.

CORPORATE INSOLVENCY

**6.38** If a family company becomes insolvent, then there are various legal procedures whereby the running of the company may be entrusted to parties other than its directors. Such a person will usually be a qualified insolvency practitioner, appointed either by the court, or by the company's creditors without court sanction. A party thus appointed is empowered to run the insolvent company so as to secure the position of the creditors as far as possible.[1] The first of these procedures which is dealt with in outline below is administrative receivership.

1 These creditors may be secured or unsecured creditors, see below.

ADMINISTRATIVE RECEIVERSHIP

**6.39** Administrative receivership is an insolvency procedure, but it is not a liquidation procedure.[1] The procedure does not generally involve the intervention of the court. An administrative receiver, once appointed, may take control of all, or substantially the whole of the company's property. He is appointed by a debenture holder under the terms of the relevant debenture.[2] The security created by the debenture under which the administrative receiver is appointed takes the form of a floating charge over all, or part, of the company's assets.[3] It is possible to create a floating charge over the company's book debts.[4] In the case of *Re New Bullas Trading Ltd*[5] the Court of Appeal recognised that both a floating and fixed charge could be created by a company over its book debts. The Court of Appeal also held that uncollected debts were subject to the fixed charge, and that these debts were not subject to s 40 of the Insolvency Act 1986. This provision deals with the situation where an administrative receiver is appointed on behalf of debenture holders to enforce the security. By s 40(2) of the Act, the preferential debts of the company must be paid in priority to the claims of the debenture holders, notwithstanding that the assets subject to the charge have been realised and the proceeds are in the hands of the receiver. The effect of the above decision is that monies subject to a fixed charge will, in the circumstances noted above, not be subject to any claims by the preferential debtors of the company. The case of *Re Bullas* may therefore have given recognition to a form of fixed charge over book debts which may be classified as a defeasible fixed charge. Such a charge bites on any property within the relevant class of assets, but is no longer subject to the charge when the property is disposed of by the company. The charge shares some of the characteristics of a floating charge to this extent.

1 Where the company is wound up and ceases to exist see below para 6.68 and Chapter 3, para 3.48.
2 Insolvency Act 1986, s 29(1). A debenture may be defined as the document which creates security over a company's property in favour of the lender. For a fuller consideration of the nature of debentures see Prime & Scanlan *The Law of Private Companies* (Butterworths, 1995) Chapter 16.
3 Insolvency Act 1986, s 29(2). A floating charge is a charge on a class of assets covering both present and future assets of that class which may be acquired by the company. The class of assets must be such that they will be constantly changing in the ordinary course of the business of the company. Furthermore, until steps are taken by those interested in the charge, known as crystallisation of the charge (see para 6.48), the company may carry on its business in the ordinary way with regard to any assets within the relevant class to which the charge relates, see *Re Yorkshire Woolcombers' Association Ltd* [1903] 2 Ch 284, CA. As it is not possible for a partnership to create a floating charge over its assets, this procedure is inapplicable to partnerships.
4 *Siebe Gorman & Co Ltd v Barclays Bank Ltd* [1979] 2 Lloyd's Rep 142.
5 [1994] 1 BCLC 485.

**6.40** The family company places the debenture holders in a more favoured position than the unsecured creditors in insolvency proceedings, by creating a right for secured creditors to appoint an administrative receiver in the security contract. Institutional lenders who provide the bulk of finance to family companies will also try to engineer this situation.

**6.41** The role of the administrative receiver is defined by s 29(2) of the Insolvency Act 1986, which nevertheless does not clearly differentiate between the very distinct roles of a receiver and a manager. The former takes control of the company's assets the latter may manage the affairs of the company. It would therefore be sensible for the creditors to require the security contract to contain a power to appoint an administrative receiver with the functions of both a receiver and a manager.[1]

1 See the powers of the court to appoint an administrative receiver under the authority of a debenture holder's action under s 32 of the Insolvency Act 1986.

## CONSEQUENCES OF APPOINTMENT OF AN ADMINISTRATIVE RECEIVER

**6.42** On the appointment of an administrative receiver, the directors cease to have any authority to deal with the property of the company. They must, however, continue to carry out their other functions.[1] Furthermore, the directors may oppose the appointment of the receiver, or oppose a petition by the receiver to wind up the company.[2] The administrative receiver must supply the directors with all the information that will enable the directors to carry out their duties.

1 *Newhart Developments Ltd v Co-operative Commercial Bank Ltd* [1978] QB 814, [1978] 2 All ER 896, CA.
2 *Re Reprographic Exports (Euromat) Ltd* (1978) 122 Sol Jo 400.

## THE RECEIVER'S POWERS

**6.43** The administrative receiver may require the directors of the company to give to him a statement of the affairs of the company.[1] Any statement of affairs should set out the following:

(a) the company's assets, debts and liabilities;
(b) details of the company's creditors;
(c) securities held by the creditors in respect of the assets of the company and the dates when they were given.

1 Insolvency Act 1986, s 47.

## THE RECEIVER'S DUTIES

**6.44** Within three months of his appointment, the administrative receiver is obliged to prepare a report for the company's creditors.[1] The report should set out the following:

(a) the events which led to his appointment;
(b) the disposal or intended disposal of the assets subject to the charge, and the carrying on, or intended carrying on of the company's business;
(c) the sums payable to the chargees who appointed him, together with the sums outstanding as preferential debts;
(d) the sums likely to be available to other creditors including unsecured creditors.

The report should also include a summary of the statement of affairs of the company, together with a summary of the receiver's comments on the statement, if the receiver has prepared one.[2]

1 Though the court may extend this time limit: Insolvency Act 1986, s 48.
2 Ibid s 48(5).

**6.45** Copies of the report must be sent within three months to the following persons:

(a) the Registrar of Companies;
(b) the trustees for secured creditors;

(c) all secured and unsecured creditors if the administrative receiver knows their addresses.[1]

The administrative receiver may, after preparation of the report, either summon a meeting of the unsecured creditors, and make copies of the report available to them;[2] or he may state in the report that he intends to apply to the court for directions that no such meeting be held.[3]

1 As an alternative, the administrative receiver may publish a notice stating an address to which unsecured creditors may write for free copies of the report, Insolvency Act 1986, s 48(2).
2 The company must not be in liquidation.
3 Insolvency Act 1986, s 48(3)(b).

**6.46** Unsecured creditors have the power to form a committee of creditors in any meeting.[1] The court has power to order that the receiver sees any relevant company books, records or papers.[2] Directors or other persons connected with the company are obliged to meet the administrative receiver and to give to him any information concerning the company which he may reasonably require.[3]

1 Insolvency Act 1986, s 49. The committee may require the receiver to furnish it with information.
2 Ibid s 234(1) and (2).
3 Insolvency Act 1986, s 234(1) and s 235.

## ADMINISTRATIVE RECEIVERSHIPS AND COMPANY CONTRACTS

**6.47** Any contract made between a company and a third party remains enforceable after the appointment of the administrative receiver.[1] The receiver is regarded as the agent of the company with respect to contracts of employment. Any contracts of employment are not therefore terminated by the appointment of a receiver.[2] If the administrative receiver decides that the company cannot be maintained as a going concern, he should dismiss the employees. The receiver should ensure that the selection procedure for dismissal is fair. Since the adoption of the contracts of employment by the receiver will render him personally liable on those contracts, the receiver is given 14 days after his appointment where he can repudiate the company's employment contracts without incurring personal liability. After this period, any payment of salaries will be construed as an adoption of those contracts.[3] The family company is no different from any other private limited company in this respect, if the employees are also family members, this will not prevent the receiver from seeking to dismiss them provided he can ensure that the company survives or at least is in a position to satisfy the debts and obligations which derive from the debenture and under which he was appointed as receiver.

1 *Freevale Ltd v Metrostore (Holdings) Ltd* [1984] Ch 199, [1984] 1 All ER 495.
2 *Griffiths v Secretary of State for Social Services* [1974] QB 468, [1973] 3 All ER 1184. Cf the position of a court-appointed receiver. *Reid v Explosives Co Ltd* (1887) 19 QBD 264, CA.
3 *Re Paramount Airways Ltd (No 3)* [1994] BCC 172, CA. The receiver is nevertheless entitled to an indemnity: Insolvency Act 1986, s 44 as amended by the Insolvency Act 1994, s 2.

## PRIORITY OF DEBTS

**6.48** The administrative receiver must satisfy certain debts and obligations of the company out of the company assets which he takes into possession in a strict order of priority. Before satisfying the obligations owed by the company to the chargees of the security contract[1] which appointed him, he must satisfy the following:

(a) preferential debts,[2]
(b) any third parties' rights in the company assets in the possession of the receiver, but only in relation to rights created in those assets prior to the crystallisation of the floating charge.[3] Crystallisation is the process whereby a floating charge over the relevant class of the company's assets is converted to a fixed charge over those same assets. In the case of most family companies this is the effective end of the business undertaking.[4]

1 That is the debenture.
2 The nature of these debts has been considered above at para 6.18. See Insolvency Act 1986, s 40.
3 Under the Insolvency Act 1986, s 43, the receiver can, where he has property in his possession which is subject to prior charges apply to the court for an order authorising him to dispose of the property free from any such charges. The proceeds must in such cases first go in satisfying these obligations.
4 It lies outside the scope of this book to consider the circumstances where crystallisation may take place. Apart from the appointment of an administrative receiver by a chargee of a debenture, crystallisation may take place in the following circumstances:
 (a) where the company goes into liquidation;
 (b) on the appointment of an administrative receiver by another chargee;
 (c) on the levy of execution or distress on the assets of the company;
 (d) the company becoming unable to pay its debts within the meaning of the Insolvency Act 1986;
 (e) if the company ceases to carry on business;
 (f) if the chargee gives notice to the company converting the floating charge to a fixed charge. This requires an express provision in the debenture documentation.

## ADMINISTRATION

**6.49** Administration of a company, including a family company, follows on from the making by the court of an administration order. The nature of the order has been considered in the context of a family partnership.[1] The principal function of an administrator is to seek, if possible, to nurse the company back to financial health. The parties who may seek an administration order include the directors, the creditors of the company, or a supervisor of a voluntary arrangement.[2]

1 See para 6.30 onwards above.
2 Insolvency Act 1986, s 7(4)(b), s 8(2) and (13).

**6.50** During the subsistence of an administration order, the company's business is managed by the court-appointed administrator. The court must not make an administration order unless it is satisfied that the company is or is likely to become unable to pay its debts.[1] Furthermore, the company must not be in liquidation.[2] The court can only make an administration order if it thinks the order would be likely to achieve one or more of the purposes set out in para 6.31.[3]

1 Insolvency Act 1986, s 8(1)(a).
2 Ibid s 8(4).
3 These purposes have been set out above within the context of an administration order made in respect of a partnership but are equally applicable to an administration order made in respect of a company.

**6.51** Where a petition for an administration order is made by a creditor, the court must consider the balance of hardship between enabling the creditor to achieve a more advantageous realisation of company assets so as to secure the debt owed to him or it, and the position of the director/shareholder where the company may be his principal source of livelihood.[1]

[1] A most pertinent consideration in the case of the family company see *Re SCL Building Services Ltd* [1990] BCLC 98.

**6.52** An administration order cannot be made if an administrative receiver has already been called in, unless the chargee consents.[1] It is therefore common practice for institutional lenders, in lending to a company, to seek to obtain not only a fixed charge over the company's assets but also to seek a floating charge over a class of the company's assets. This will enable the creditor to appoint an administrative receiver and thereby thwart any administration order that may be sought in respect of the company by the directors or any other creditor of the company, particularly unsecured creditors.[2] Such a procedure is not available to the creditor where the business is a partnership, since it is not possible for a partnership to create a floating charge over its assets.

[1] Or the court is satisfied that if an order were made the relevant floating charge would be discharged, avoided or declared invalid by the court (Insolvency Act 1986, ss 238–240 and ss 245 and 9(3)). As for the circumstances where the administrative receiver is called in on the crystallisation of the charge see para 6.48.
[2] *Re Croftbell Ltd* [1990] BCLC 844.

## THE FUNCTIONS AND PURPOSE OF THE ADMINISTRATOR

**6.53** The administrator must prepare a statement of the proposals for achieving the aims and purposes of the administration order[1] within three months of his appointment.[2] A copy of the statement must be sent to the Registrar and to the company's creditors, before a summoning a meeting of the creditors to consider and approve the statement.

[1] These have been noted above in respect of an administration order made with regard to a partnership. See also the Insolvency Act 1986, s 18.
[2] Although this period may be extended.

## CREDITORS' MEETING

**6.54** The proposals in the statement must be approved by the creditors' meeting before they can be implemented.[1] Only unsecured creditors can vote at the meeting and the votes are calculated by reference to the value of the debts owed to them by the company. The meeting thus determines the function of the administrator. If the meeting does not approve the proposals, then the court may discharge the administration order.[2] There is some protection for the interests of the shareholders of the company. They may apply to the court[3] for an order regulating the administrator's management of the company on the grounds that the administrator's present or even future actions are, or would be, unfairly prejudicial to their interests. However, this is a remedy that the court would be unlikely to grant even in the case of a family company. After the creditors' meeting, the creditors may form a creditors' committee.[4] This body may oversee the actions of the administrator, and should be kept informed of his actions. The administrator can be compelled to attend a meeting of this committee.[5]

1 Insolvency Act 1986, s 24(1). See *Re Consumer and Industrial Press Ltd (No 2)* (1987) 4 BCC 72.
2 Ibid s 24(5)
3 Insolvency Act 1986, s 27.
4 Ibid s 26.
5 Insolvency Act 1986, s 26(2).

POWERS OF THE ADMINISTRATOR

**6.55** The powers of the administrator are the same as those of the directors of the company. He may therefore do all things which are necessary for the management of the affairs of the company.[1]

1 Insolvency Act 1986, s 14 and Sch 1.

**6.56** The administrator in exercising his powers does so as an agent of the company.[1] He has no statutory liability in respect of company contracts. The administrator may carry out the following functions:

(a) the calling of meetings of shareholders or creditors of the company;
(b) the disposing of company property which is subject to a charge which was originally a floating charge, as if the property were not subject to a charge.[2] The relevant chargees will, however, enjoy the same priority in any property which represents the proceeds of disposal.
(c) the administrator may dispose of property subject to a charge under the same circumstances and under the same conditions as an administrative receiver under s 43 of the Insolvency Act 1986.[3]
(d) he may prepare statements of affairs under s 22 of the Insolvency Act 1986.[4]

1 Insolvency Act 1986, s 14.
2 Ibid s 15.
3 See para 6.48 above.
4 This is the same procedure as the preparation of a statement by an administrative receiver under s 47, noted in para 6.43 above.

PRIORITY OF PAYMENT OF DEBTS

**6.57** The debts and liabilities incurred by the administrator during the administration including the administrator's expenses, must be met out of the company's assets which are in the control and possession of the administrator. The administrator's expenses have priority over the expenses of any administrative receiver which are payable out of company assets subject to the charge under which the receiver was appointed.[1] Preferential debts owed by the company under contracts of employment enjoy the same priority.[2] As in the case of an administrative receiver, the administrator has a 14-day period from the date of his appointment when he will not be regarded as having adopted any contracts of employment where the company is an employer.[3] However, an administrator does not incur personal liability in respect of any such contracts which he adopts even after that period unlike an administrative receiver.

1 Insolvency Act 1986, s 19.
2 Ibid s 19(6), inserted by the Insolvency Act 1994, s 1(4), but limited to sums payable in respect of services rendered during the administrator's tenure of office.
3 *Re Ferranti International plc* [1994] 4 All ER 300.

**6.58** During the subsistence of the administration order, the secured creditors of the company cannot, except with leave of the court, enforce their security by recourse to any legal process.[1]

1 Insolvency Act 1986, s 11. *Re Atlantic Computer Systems plc* [1992] Ch 505 at 541–544, CA.

**6.59** The company cannot be wound up during the continuance of an administration order.[1] Under s 10(3) of the Insolvency Act 1986, if an administration order is presented at a time when an administrative receiver has been appointed under a security contract, then the period of immunity from other insolvency procedures which would normally last until the winding up of the company cannot commence unless and until the party or parties who appointed the receiver consent to the making of the administration order.

1 Insolvency Act 1986, s 10.

## VOLUNTARY ARRANGEMENTS

**6.60** A voluntary arrangement[1] is invariably but not always invoked when the company is insolvent. A proposal for a voluntary arrangement need only be reported to the court. A voluntary arrangement is an approved proposal, determined at a meeting of the company's unsecured creditors and a meeting of its shareholders. A three-quarters majority of the unsecured creditors by value of credit must approve the proposed voluntary arrangement at the creditors' meeting. The arrangement then binds all of the company's creditors. The arrangement takes the form of a composition in satisfaction of the company's debts or a scheme of arrangement of the company's affairs.

1 The nature of a voluntary arrangement has been considered within the context of a partnership, see para 6.27 above.

**6.61** A proposal for a voluntary arrangement can be made by the directors if the company is neither in liquidation nor subject to the administration procedure.[1] The insolvency practitioner nominated by the directors to administer the arrangement must submit a report to the court as to whether the proposal should be put to the meeting of the company's creditors and shareholders within 28 days of his appointment.[2] The directors must supply the practitioner with a statement of the company's affairs, together with any other information he requires.[3] If in his opinion, the proposal should be put to any meetings, then he must summon meetings of all the creditors and shareholders of the company at a time, date and place proposed in the report.[4]

1 Insolvency Act 1986, s 1.
2 Ibid s 2.
3 Insolvency Act 1986, s 2(3).
4 Ibid s 3(10).

**6.62** Despite the fact that the voluntary arrangement may have been proposed so as to secure a more advantageous realisation of company assets, both for the creditors of the company and its shareholders, the proposal may encourage creditors to seek to have the company wound up. The directors may also wish to present an administration order to prevent this from happening.[1]

1 See para 6.49 above.

**6.63** Where a company is in liquidation, or under administration, the liquidator or administrator may propose a composition or scheme of arrangement in respect of the company which is to be supervised by either the liquidator or administrator.[1] Either of these parties may summon a meeting of the company's creditors and a meeting of the shareholders, without the approval of the court.[2] The procedure for initiation and execution of the composition or scheme of arrangement in the above cases then follows the procedure for voluntary arrangements where the company is not in liquidation or administration, which has been noted at para 6.60 above.

1 Insolvency Act 1986, s 1(3).
2 Ibid s 3(2).

## APPROVAL OF A PROPOSAL FOR A VOLUNTARY ARRANGEMENT

**6.64** The purpose of meetings of the company's shareholders and creditors, is to determine whether to approve the proposal for the composition or scheme of arrangement. They may do so with modifications.[1] No proposal may however, deprive a secured creditor of his or its rights to enforce the security without his or its consent.[2] Neither can a proposal be adopted by the meetings which would affect the priority of any preferential debt.[3]

1 Insolvency Act 1986, s 4(1).
2 Ibid s 4(3).
3 Insolvency Act 1986, s 4(4).

**6.65** The chairman of each meeting of the creditors and the shareholders must report the results of any meeting to the court, and give notice of the results of the meeting to those whose presence was required.[1] If the meetings approve the proposal, then it takes effect as if approved solely by the creditor's meeting, and binds every one including all of the unsecured creditors. Certain persons may however, apply to the court within 28 days of the making of the reports to seek the revocation or suspension of the proposal for the composition or scheme of arrangement. The persons may include:[2]

(a) any person entitled to vote at the creditors' meeting;
(b) any shareholder entitled to vote at the members' meeting;
(c) the company liquidator; and
(d) the company administrator.

1 Insolvency Act 1986, s 4(6).
2 Ibid s 6.

**6.66** The grounds upon which the court may revoke or suspend the approved scheme or composition are:

(a) that the proposal or scheme is unfairly prejudicial to the interests of a creditor, shareholder or contributory to the company; and/or
(b) that there has been a material irregularity in the conducting of either or both meetings.[1]

The court, in revoking or suspending any approved proposal for a composition or scheme of arrangement of a company's affairs may also direct that revised proposals be put before further meetings of the company's creditors and shareholders.[2]

1 Insolvency Act 1986, s 6(7).
2 Ibid s 6(4).

**6.67** Where a proposal has been approved and the company is in liquidation, or subject to an administration order, then if no appeal is made against the proposal or it is otherwise approved by the court, the court may order the staying of the winding-up order, or discharge the administration order.[1]

1 Insolvency Act 1986, s 5(3) and (4).

## COMPULSORY LIQUIDATION

**6.68** The above procedure is invoked in respect of insolvent companies. It is also a process whereby the company may be liquidated.[1] The process is regulated by the Insolvency Act 1986. A petition to wind up a company is thus made under the Act. If the court makes the order then the winding-up is deemed to commence when the petition was presented.[2] The granting of a winding-up order is discretionary, however, a petition for the winding up[3] of an insolvent company *must* be dismissed if an administration order is made while the petition for the winding up of the company is pending.[4]

1 For the nature of liquidation see Chapter 3, para 3.48 onwards.
2 Insolvency Act 1986, s 129(2).
3 Winding up and liquidation are synonymous.
4 Insolvency Act 1986, s 11(1)(a).

## PETITIONERS

**6.69** The principal parties who may petition for the compulsory winding up of an insolvent company are as follows:[1]

(a) any secured or unsecured creditor of the company;
(b) any contributory of the company;[2]
(c) the directors of the company;
(d) a supervisor of a voluntary arrangement;[3]
(e) an administrator of the company;
(f) an administrative receiver of the company.

All or any of the above parties may petition collectively or separately.

1 Insolvency Act 1986, s 124(1).
2 Ibid s 79. See below.
3 Insolvency Act 1986, s 7(4)(b)

**6.70** The court will order the compulsory winding-up of an insolvent company if the company is unable to pay its debts.[1] Where a creditor has served a statutory demand for payment of the debt owed to him or it under s 123(1)(a), he or it must wait three weeks before he can present a petition for the winding up of the company. This however, gives more than adequate time for the company's assets to be dissipated for the benefit of secured creditors, or even to encourage the company to bury itself in more debt in a vain attempt to escape the consequences of the serving of the statutory demand.[2]

1 Insolvency Act 1986, s 123(1), (2). These grounds have been considered above in the context of the insolvent partnership see para 6.4, n 1.
2 *Taylors Industrial Flooring Ltd v M & H Plant Hire (Manchester) Ltd* [1990] BCLC 216 at 219, CA.

**6.71** Where the court makes a winding-up order in respect of a company, the official receiver effectively becomes the liquidator. Where the winding-up order is made immediately on the discharge of an administration order, or where there is a supervisor of an existing voluntary arrangement, the administrator or supervisor may be appointed by the court as the liquidator of the company.[1] In these cases the creditors' meeting can remove the liquidator.

1 Insolvency Act 1986, s 140(1) and (2).

**6.72** The official receiver as the liquidator must determine if the company requires investigation. He may also have the company dissolved[1] if he considers the assets of the company as being insufficient to cover the costs of liquidation and investigation of the company's affairs. Either the official receiver, or 25% of the creditors of the company, (calculated by value of the debts of the company), may request the summoning of meetings of both the creditors and shareholders of the company, which may then nominate a liquidator to replace the official receiver.[2] If the two meetings select different nominees for the post, the appointment of the creditors' meeting will have priority.[3]

1 Insolvency Act 1986, s 202.
2 Ibid s 236(4) and (5).
3 Insolvency Act 1986, s 139(2) and (3).

## LIQUIDATION COMMITTEE

**6.73** The meetings of the creditors and shareholders may establish a liquidation committee.[1] The function of this committee is to assist and supervise the work of the liquidator.[2]

1 Insolvency Act 1986, s 141(1).
2 Ibid s 167(1)(a).

## POWERS AND DUTIES OF THE LIQUIDATOR

**6.74** The principal function of the liquidator in an insolvent liquidation of the company, is to gather in and to realise the assets of the company.[1] The powers and functions of the directors effectively cease. The liquidator takes the company's undertaking[2] into his possession and control. The directors may, however, appeal against the winding up order and the appointment of the liquidator.[3] Subject to the above, the effect of the winding up order may be to remove the directors permanently from office.

1 Insolvency Act 1986, s 143(1).
2 *Re Farrow's Bank Ltd* [1921] 2 Ch 164, CA.
3 *Re Diamond Fuel Co* (1879) 13 Ch D 400, CA.

## PRIORITY OF PAYMENT

**6.75** After the expenses of gathering in and realising the company assets have been satisfied, together with the expenses of the liquidator, the liquidator must then pay, in order of priority:

(a) the preferential debts of the company;[1]
(b) the unsecured creditors.[2]

1 See para 6.18 for a consideration of the nature of preferential debts. Section 175 and Sch 6 of the Insolvency Act 1986 sets out the full list of preferential debts.
2 The debts which the company owes to secured creditors will of course be satisfied out of the assets subject to the security contract.

**6.76** In most family companies subject to a winding-up order, the assets of the company are likely to be insufficient to satisfy the obligations owed to all the unsecured creditors in full. If any assets are however, available, the creditors will receive pro rata a sum proportionate to the debt that the company owes to them. If the unsecured creditors can be paid in full then any sums remaining can be used by the liquidator, subject to a court order to satisfy any debts owing to a party who has been ordered to be a contributory to the company assets.[1] The liquidator may also pay post-liquidation interest on any such sums.

1 Under s 213 and s 214 of the Companies Act 1985, see paras 6.88 and 6.90 below.

**6.77** The next debts to be satisfied are any sums paid by the company to purchase its own shares, where a contract was entered into by the company prior to the winding up. Post-liquidation interest may also be paid on such sums. Any surplus of company assets left after satisfaction of the above may be used to satisfy debts owed to members or past members of the company incurred before the commencement of liquidation.[1] The most common example of such a liability is dividends which were declared before the liquidation of the company but which remain unpaid. Post liquidation interest may be paid on any such sums paid in respect of this category of company debt.

1 Insolvency Act 1986, s 74(2)(f).

**6.78** After satisfaction of the above debts, the liquidator must then apply any surplus assets or their proceeds in satisfying the expenses of summoning and holding any meeting of the contributories. If there is any surplus following the meeting of this liability, it may be distributed to the shareholders.[1] In these cases the company is not insolvent and the liquidation, though compulsory, is not an insolvency procedure.

1 Companies Act 1985, s 154.

## EXAMINATION OF TRANSACTIONS

**6.79** Where an insolvent company goes into compulsory liquidation, or is subject to an administration order, the only assets available to the liquidator or administrator to satisfy the company's creditors are those the company has at the onset of the insolvency. In order to increase the pool of assets available to satisfy creditors of the company, the court may in certain circumstances require on the application of the liquidator or administrator, that transactions of the company involving the assets of the company be re-opened. The circumstances in which such transactions may be re-opened are set out in the Insolvency Act 1986. It is not possible to examine these provisions in detail in this chapter.[1] The principal provisions will however, be set out below. It must be emphasised that these statutory provisions will only operate if the company is in the course of being liquidated, or is the subject of an administration order. It is not enough that the company is insolvent. Furthermore, even if a transaction diminishes the assets of the company, the transaction cannot be set aside under any of the statutory provisions if at the time of the transaction the company is able to pay its debts as and when they fall due. If the transaction causes the company to become insolvent, or at the time of the transaction, the company is insolvent and goes into liquidation, or an administration order is made within a time prescribed by the relevant statutory provision, then the transaction may be avoided. The principal statutory provisions applicable to a family company are set out below.

1 See Prime & Scanlan T*he Law of Private Limited Companies*, Chapter 22 for a more detailed consideration of these provisions.

TRANSACTIONS AT AN UNDERVALUE – INSOLVENCY ACT 1986, s 238

**6.80** For the purposes of the above section, a transfer of company assets which includes a gift,[1] may be set aside if the transaction was entered into within the relevant time. The relevant time is defined by s 240 of the Insolvency Act 1986 as:

> 'Where the transaction is entered into by the company with a person connected with the company (otherwise than by reason of employment) the relevant time is within two years of the onset of the company's insolvency, or in any other case, the relevant time is at a time between the presentation of a petition for the making of an administration order in relation to the company and the making of such an order on that petition.'

The circumstances in which a transaction will not be within the relevant time, or otherwise subject to s 238 have been noted above in para 6.79. Where the section applies to a transaction, the court may make any order it sees fit, including an order restoring any property to the company.[2] The court will not make an order if it satisfied that the company entered into the transaction in good faith and for the purposes of carrying on its business and, at the time of the transaction, there were reasonable grounds for believing the transaction would benefit the company.[3]

1 For example, between the company and a spouse of one of the company directors/shareholders.
2 Insolvency Act 1986, s 241.
3 Ibid s 238(5).

PREFERENCES – INSOLVENCY ACT 1986, s 239

**6.81** The statutory provision governing preferences, s 239 of the Insolvency Act 1986, is intended to uphold the principle of equal ranking and priority between classes of creditor. It applies in broadly the same circumstances as s 238. Under s 239, where the company at the relevant time[1] has given a preference to a creditor, surety or guarantor, the liquidator or administrator of the company may apply for an order under the section. The orders the court can make are set out in s 241. The purpose of any order is to restore the company to the position it would have enjoyed if the preference had never been given.

1 This is the same as in s 238, see para 6.80 above. In addition, where the preference is given to a party not connected with the company (otherwise than by reason of employment) the relevant time for the giving of the preference is within a period of six months, which ends with the onset of the insolvency of the company, see s 240(3).

## EXTORTIONATE CREDIT TRANSACTIONS – INSOLVENCY ACT 1986, s 244

**6.82** The liquidator or administrator of the company may seek an order under s 244, inter alia, to set aside an extortionate credit transaction entered into by the company.[1] The court may make an order with respect to any such transaction, if it was made within three years, ending with the day on which the administration order was made, or the company went into liquidation. An extortionate credit transaction is a transaction which grossly contravenes ordinary principles of fair trading.[2] The transaction must therefore be oppressive and not merely burdensome.

1 Insolvency Act, s 249(4) sets out the orders the court may make under s 244.
2 Ibid s 244(3).

## FLOATING CHARGES FOR PAST VALUE – INSOLVENCY ACT 1986, s 245

**6.83** By virtue of s 245 of the Insolvency Act 1986, a floating charge created over a company's assets or undertaking at the relevant time, will be invalid unless the following conditions are satisfied, that the aggregate of:

(a) The value of so much of the consideration for the creation of the charge as consists of money paid, or goods or services supplied and is furnished at or after the creation of the charge and forms part of the same transaction.
(b) The value of so much of that consideration as consists of the discharge or reduction at the same time as, or after the creation of the charge of any debts of the company, and the amount of any interest payable on any amounts falling within either of the above circumstances and in pursuance of any agreement under which the money was paid, or the goods or services were supplied or the debt discharged or reduced.[1]

1 Insolvency Act 1986, s 245(6).

**6.84** The relevant time for the purposes of s 245 is if the charge is created:

(a) in favour of a person connected with the company, within a period of two years ending with the onset of insolvency;[1]
(b) in the case of a charge created by the company in favour of any other person within a period of 12 months ending with the onset of insolvency;[2] and
(c) in either of the above cases, if the charge is created at a time between the presentation of a petition for the making of an administration order in relation to the company and the making of such an order on that petition.

1 Insolvency Act 1986, s 245(3).
2 Ibid.

**6.85** Where the company creates a floating charge over its assets in favour of a person not connected with the company, the time of the transaction will not be regarded in any circumstances as being within the ambit of the relevant time unless the company is unable to pay its debts at the time, or as a consequence of that transaction.[1]

1 Insolvency Act 1986, s 245(4).

## DISPOSITIONS – INSOLVENCY ACT 1986, s 127

**6.86** Section 127 of the Insolvency Act 1986 provides that:

> 'any transfer of shares or alteration in the status of the company's members, made after the commencement of the winding up is, unless the court orders otherwise void.'

## TRANSACTIONS DEFRAUDING CREDITORS – INSOLVENCY ACT 1986, s 423

**6.87** Under s 423, where a company enters into a transaction with a third party at an undervalue for the purpose of putting assets beyond the reach of a person making or entitled to make a claim against the company, or otherwise prejudicing the interests of such a claimant, the court may, inter alia, make an order restoring the status quo. The section may apply irrespective of whether the company is the subject of an administration order, or in the process of insolvent compulsory liquidation.

### Fraudulent trading – Insolvency Act 1986, s 213

**6.88** A party[1] who is found to have been a knowing participant in the carrying on of the company's business with intent to defraud creditors, or the creditors of any other person, or for any other fraudulent purpose, may be held to be liable under s 213 to make such contributions to the company's assets as the court thinks proper. Such a contributory may, where he is a director of the company, be subject to a disqualification order under s 10 of the Company Directors Disqualification Act 1986. The director may therefore be disqualified from holding the office of director of a company for a specific period of time.

1 Generally the director of a family company.

**6.89** A declaration by the court under s 213 may only be made while the company is going through the process of liquidation. It is the liquidator of the company who applies for the declaration. A director may act with intent to defraud and for a fraudulent purpose only where his actions involve 'actual dishonesty importing, according to current notions of fair trading among commercial men, real commercial blame'.[1] It is therefore dangerous for the directors of a family company who are aware that the company is unable to pay its debts, to continue to obtain credit, in the hope that they may be able to turn the financial corner. In such cases the directors run the risk of being made the subject, in the event of the company being wound up, of a court order that they contribute personally to the company's assets. It may be said however, that fraud is difficult to establish. Furthermore, the liquidator may find that the directors have no realisable assets.[2] Accordingly, a liquidator will rarely have recourse to s 213.

1 *Re Patrick and Lyon Ltd* [1933] Ch 786 per Maugham J.
2 See para 6.97 below.

## WRONGFUL TRADING – INSOLVENCY ACT 1986, s 214

**6.90** Under the above provision the court may declare a director of a family company liable to contribute to the assets of the company on its winding up. The court will only make such a declaration if it is satisfied that the director knew, or ought to have concluded that the company had no reasonable prospect of not going into insolvent liquidation, and did not take every step that ought to have been taken to minimise loss to the company's creditors. Accordingly, when the company goes into liquidation, it must have insufficient assets to meet its debts and liabilities. It is up to the liquidator to seek such a declaration.

**6.91** In determining the standard of behaviour of a director, and their knowledge of the company's financial situation for the purposes of s 214, the court will impose a minimum objective standard on the relevant party as possessed by a reasonably diligent person, with the knowledge, skill and experience that could reasonably be expected of a person carrying out the function of a director of the company, the standard of behaviour is variable however, for where a director possess greater experience, skill or knowledge than that of a reasonably diligent person, the standard applied to the director in determining his potential liability under s 214 is that actually possessed by him.[1] The standard of behaviour that may generally be imposed on the average director of a family company will, it is suggested be a low one.

1 Insolvency Act 1986, s 214(4) and (5).

**6.92** In theory, s 214 places even greater pressure on directors than s 213 to cease trading, and to put the company into compulsory liquidation, if the company becomes insolvent. The consequences of not doing so are that a director may be liable to contribute financially on the winding up of the company. A director may also be subject to the provisions of the Company Directors Disqualification Act, which have been noted above in the context of s 213. Although a declaration under s 214 does not require proof of fraudulent conduct, the use of the section by the liquidator will in practice be limited. In the case of many family companies, the insolvency of the company involves the bankruptcy of the directors.[1] In these cases, the liquidator will be wasting his time and the substance of the company in seeking to increase the assets available to satisfy the unsecured creditors of the company by recourse to s 214, since he will be seeking contributions to the company's assets from men of straw. Conversely, it would be sensible for the directors of a family company, which becomes insolvent to seek the immediate advice of an experienced qualified insolvency practitioner, this may avoid any possible liability under s 214.

1 See para 6.97 below.

## MISFEANCE PROCEEDINGS – INSOLVENCY ACT 1986, s 212

**6.93** Under s 212 of the Insolvency Act 1986, the liquidator may institute proceedings to recover property which was formerly property of the company, and which has been misapplied by any party who formed or managed the company. The persons who may therefore be held liable under such misfeasance proceedings will include:

(a) any party who is or who was an officer of the company, usually a director or former director;
(b) any party who has acted as liquidator, administrator, or administrative receiver of the company;
(c) any party who is, or has been concerned or involved in the promotion, formation or management of the company.

**6.94** The grounds upon which misfeasance proceedings may be brought, are that the relevant party has either misapplied, or retained, or become accountable for any money, or other form of property of the company, or the party has been guilty of misfeasance, or a breach of a fiduciary or other duty, in relation to the company or its creditors. Thus, such proceedings may be used to recover dividends from directors that have not been paid out of distributable profits.[1]

1 *Re National Funds Assurance Co* (1878) 10 Ch D 118.

## CONCLUSION

**6.95** The various insolvency procedures applicable to the family partnership and the family company considered in this chapter illustrate that the selection of either form of business structure by a family business will not prevent the personal bankruptcy of the participants in the enterprise. The supposed disadvantage of the partnership as governed by the Partnership Act 1890 as a medium for the family business is that its members cannot invoke the protection of limited liability. The personal separate estates of the members are available to satisfy the creditors of the business in the event of the insolvency of the enterprise. Nevertheless, the application of insolvency procedures such as the winding-up of a partnership as an unregistered company under the Insolvent Partnerships Order 1994, recognises the separation of the joint estate of the partnership from that of the respective estates of the family members. Furthermore, the application of such insolvency procedures as the administration order and the voluntary arrangement to the partnership, although originally devised for the company, has reduced the distinction between the unincorporated partnership and the company at least as regards the insolvency of such business enterprises.

**6.96** The commonly held view that the private limited company enables the participants in the enterprise to protect their separate estates in the event of the insolvency of the business does not bear close scrutiny. The liquidator on the winding up of a family company may seek to hold the directors/shareholders liable to contribute to the assets of the company in order to satisfy the unsecured debts and liabilities incurred by the company. These procedures also reduce the distinction between the separate estates of the participants of the business and the assets of the company, and render the private company a more financially transparent medium than case law would suggest.[1]

1 *Salomon v A Salomon & Co Ltd* [1897] AC 22, HL.

**6.97** It is however, the practicality of running and financing a modern business that reduces the effectiveness of the private limited company as a means by which family members can operate an enterprise without risking their personal estates. Financial institutions, in lending to a family business, may seek a company form because they will be able to secure both a fixed and floating charge on the assets of the company. They may have recourse to administrative receivership in the event of the company defaulting on its liabilities. However, these institutions will also usually insist, as a condition of lending to the family company, that the directors/shareholders enter into personal guarantees and give security on their personal property. The insolvency and compulsory winding-up of the family company therefore frequently involves the simultaneous personal bankruptcy of the participants in the business. The selection therefore of either the partnership or the private limited company as the appropriate medium for the members of a family business, to conduct their enterprise on the grounds of protection of its participants from personal bankruptcy, is in practical terms a neutral decision. Neither a partnership or a private limited company having a decisive advantage in this regard. The advantages and disadvantages of forming either business medium are in these circumstances finely balanced.

# Index

**Accounts**
  abbreviated, form of,
    dispensing with laying accounts, 1.18
    medium-sized companies, 1.16
    small companies, 1.17
  accounting requirements,
    exemptions and exceptions to, 1.12–1.15
    medium-sized companies, 1.13–1.15
    small companies, 1.13–1.15
  comparative costs, 1.10–1.11
  dispensing with laying with, 1.18
  partnership,
    adjustment of, 3.78–3.81
    generally, 2.13
**Administrative receivership.** See INSOLVENCY
**Advance corporation tax**
  qualifying distribution, 1.7
**Agreement**
  partnership, 2.4–2.9 5.8
  shareholder,
    contents, 2.64–2.65
    minority shareholder, protection of, 5.53–5.54
    standard provisions contained in, 2.65
    use of, 2.63 2.66
**Ante-nuptial settlement**
  variation of, 3.44
**Arbitration**
  partnership agreement, clause in, 2.31
**Articles of association**
  management of business, 2.36
**Auditor**
  appointment of, 1.19

**Bankruptcy**
  partner, of, 2.22

**Consent order**
  divorce proceedings, relating to, 3.46
**Control**
  concept of, 5.32
  fraud on minority by those in, 5.32
**Controlling shareholder**
  death of, 4.4–4.8
**Corporate insolvency.** See INSOLVENCY

**Corporation tax**
  current rates, 1.7
**Costs**
  accounts, 1.10–1.11
  comparative, 1.9–1.11
**Court**
  dissolution of partnership by order of, 3.73
**Creditors' voluntary liquidation.** See
    WINDING UP

**Death**
  controlling shareholder, of, 4.4–4.8
  creditors of partnership, effect on, 4.12–4.13
  generally, 4.1 4.37
  inheritance problems arising on, 4.1
  life interests,
    family company, 4.34–4.35
    partnership, 4.32–4.33
  partner, of, 2.18–2.19 4.9–4.11
  partnership,
    beneficiaries, 4.18–4.20
    bequest of partnership share, 4.27–4.31
    creditors of, 4.12–4.13
    debts incurred after partner's death, 4.14
    life interests, 4.32–4.33
    loans to, 4.21–4.26
    personal representatives admitted as partners, 4.15–4.17
    separate creditors, 4.18–4.20
  problems arising on, 4.1 4.37
  shareholder in family company, of, 4.2–4.3
  winding up on death of member, 4.36
**Debts**
  priority of. See INSOLVENCY
**Deregulation**
  new regime for, 1.20
**Directors**
  appointment of, 2.34
  authority of, 2.62
  duties of, 2.39
  fiduciary duties, 2.40–2.41
  financial provision, 2.50
  individual shareholders, duties to, 2.43–2.45
  managing director, 2.38

115

**Directors** – *contd*
  matrimonial disputes, 3.36–3.40
  minority shareholders,
    action against directors, 5.30–5.31
    duties relating to, 5.29
  powers of, 2.35
  profiting, rules against, 2.42
  removal of, 2.53–2.57
  remuneration, effect of divorce on, 3.19
  responsibilities, 2.34
  retirement, 2.52
  termination of office, 2.51
**Discrimination**
  partnership or company, 1.30
**Dissolution.** *See* WINDING UP
**Dividends**
  divorce, effect of, 3.20
**Divorce**
  ante-nuptial settlement, variation of, 3.44
  business as family property, 3.2–3.4
  consent orders, 3.46
  directors' remuneration, 3.19
  dividends, 3.20
  family property, business as, 3.2–3.4
  generally, 3.1 3.47 3.84
  lump sum payments,
    court not granting order, 3.41–3.42
    generally, 3.14
    raising funds, 3.15–3.18
  maintenance payments, taxation of, 3.11–3.13
  matrimonial disputes, 3.36–3.40
  partnership,
    assignment of share, 3.31–3.35
    increase of drawings by partner, 3.21
    purchase of partner's share, 3.28–3.29
  periodical payments,
    secured, 3.8–3.10
    unsecured, 3.7
  post-nuptial settlement, variation of, 3.44
  property order, transfer and settlement of, 3.43
  purchase by company of its own shares,
    effect of, 3.22–3.24
    fiscal consequences of acquisition, 3.25–3.27
  raising funds, 3.15–3.18
  remuneration of directors, 3.19
  sale of property, orders for, 3.45
  sale of shares to third party, 3.30
  secured payments, 3.8–3.10
  settlement,
    ante-nuptial, variation of, 3.44
    generally, 3.5–3.6
    post-nuptial, variation of, 3.44
  settlement of property order, 3.43
  tax implications, 3.11–3.13
  third party, sale of shares to, 3.30
  transfer of property order, 3.43
  unsecured payments, 3.7
  winding up of company on. *See* WINDING UP

**Family business**
  concept of, 1.1
  meaning, 1.1
**Finance**
  directors, provision for, 2.50
  partnership or company, 1.6
**Fixed charge**
  institutional lender, use by, 1.6
**Floating charge**
  institutional lender, use by, 1.6
  past value, for, 6.83–6.85
**Formation of business**
  accounts and reports, form of,
    comparative costs, 1.10–1.11
    deregulation, new regime for, 1.20
    dispensing with laying accounts, 1.18
    medium-sized companies, 1.16
    small companies, 1.17
  company auditors, 1.19
  comparative costs,
    accounts, 1.10–1.11
    generally, 1.9
  concept of family business, 1.1
  discrimination, 1.30
  exemptions and exceptions,
    generally, 1.12
    medium-sized companies, 1.13–1.15
    small companies, 1.13–1.15
  financing business, 1.6
  fiscal advantages, 1.7–1.8
  generally, 1.1–1.3 1.33
  hiving off parts of business, 1.23–1.26
  incorporation,
    generally, 1.21
    selling of business in whole or in part, 1.22
  limited liability, 1.4–1.5
  mergers, 1.27–1.29
  restraint of trade, 1.31–1.32
  selling of business in whole or in part, 1.22
  social welfare legislation, 1.30
**Fraud**
  control, concept of, 5.32
  maintaining derivative action, 5.33–5.36
**Fraudulent trading**
  declaration by court, 6.89
  disqualification of director, 6.88

**Good faith**
  partners acting in, 5.14–5.15

**Hiving off**
  partnership or company, 1.23–1.26

**Illness**
  partner, of, 2.29–2.30
**Income tax**
  higher rate, 1.7
**Incorporation**
  partnership or company, 1.21–1.22
  selling of business in whole or in part, 1.22
**Indemnities**
  partners, relating to, 2.17

**Injunction**
minority partner seeking, 5.16–5.18
**Insolvency**
corporate,
administration order, 6.49–6.52
administrative receiver,
appointment of, 6.39–6.40
consequences of appointment, 6.42
duties of, 6.44–6.46
powers of, 6.43
role of, 6.41
administrator,
functions of, 6.53
powers of, 6.55–6.56
purpose of, 6.53
company contracts, administrative receivership and, 6.47
compulsory liquidation, 6.68
creditor's meeting, 6.54
dispositions, 6.86
examination of transactions, 6.79
extortionate credit transactions, 6.82
floating charges for past value, 6.83–6.85
fraudulent trading, 6.88–6.89
generally, 6.38 6.95–6.97
liquidation committee, 6.73
liquidator, powers and duties of, 6.74
misfeasance proceedings, 6.93–6.94
past value, floating charges for, 6.83–6.85
petitioners, 6.69–6.72
preferences, 6.81
priority of debts, 6.48
priority of payment of debts, 6.57–6.59 6.75–6.78
transactions at undervalue, 6.80
transactions defrauding creditors, 6.87–6.89
voluntary arrangement,
approval of proposal for, 6.64–6.67
proposal for, 6.60–6.63
wrongful trading, 6.90–6.92
partnership,
administration of estates, 6.15
administration orders, 6.30–6.37
contributory, partner as, 6.12–6.14
expenses incurred by responsible insolvency practitioner, 6.16–6.17
generally, 3.83 6.1 6.26–6.29 6.95–6.97
insolvency practitioner, expenses incurred by, 6.16–6.17
joint petition by all partners, 6.9
petition,
concurrent, winding up without, 6.4
consequences of presentation of, 6.6
joint, by all partners, 6.9
parties who may present, 6.5
presented against one or more partners, 6.10
winding up order with concurrent petition, 6.7–6.8
priority of debts,
generally, 6.25
joint estate, in, 6.18–6.22

**Insolvency** – *contd*
partnership – *contd*
priority of debts – *contd*
separate estates, in, 6.23–6.24
procedures, 6.2
unregistered company, winding up as, 6.3
winding up,
position of partners, 6.11
unregistered company, as, 6.3
without concurrent petition, 6.4
priority of debts,
administrative receiver, powers of, 6.48
insolvent partnership, 6.25
joint estate, in, 6.18–6.22
separate estates, in, 6.23–6.24
**Institutional lenders**
financing business, 1.6
**Insurance**
partnership, 2.28

**Judicial separation.** *See* DIVORCE

**Life interests**
family company, relating to, 4.34–4.35
partnership, relating to, 4.32–4.33
**Limited company**
partnership or,
accounts and reports,
abbreviated, form of, 1.16–1.18
comparative costs, 1.10–1.11
deregulation, new regime for, 1.20
dispensing with laying accounts, 1.18
exemptions and exceptions, 1.12–1.15
medium-sized companies, 1.13–1.15 1.16
small companies, 1.13–1.15 1.17
company auditors, 1.19
comparative costs, 1.9–1.11
discrimination, 1.30
financing business, 1.6
fiscal advantages, 1.7–1.8
generally, 1.1–1.3 1.33
hiving off parts of business, 1.23–1.26
incorporation, 1.21–1.22
limited liability, 1.4–1.5
mergers, 1.27–1.29
restraint of trade, 1.31–1.32
selling of business in whole or in part, 1.22
social welfare legislation, 1.30
**Limited liability**
partnership or company, 1.4–1.5
**Liquidator**
appointment of, 3.54–3.57
provisional, appointment of, 3.64
*See also* INSOLVENCY; WINDING UP
**Loans**
partnership, to, 4.21–4.26
**Lump sum payments.** *See* DIVORCE

**Maintenance payments**
taxation, 3.11–3.13

**Manager**
  appointment of, 5.19–5.21
**Managing director**
  appointment of, 2.38
**Mediation**
  partnership dispute, resolution of, 2.32
**Medium-sized companies**
  abbreviated accounts and reports, form of, 1.16
  accounting requirements, exemptions and exceptions to, 1.13–1.15
**Meetings**
  partnership, 2.12
**Members' voluntary liquidation.** *See* WINDING UP
**Mergers**
  partnership or company, 1.27–1.29
**Minority protection**
  minority shareholder,
    Companies Act 1985, s 459, 5.37–5.40
    directors,
      action against, 5.30–5.31
      duties of, 5.29
    fraud, concept of, 5.33–5.36
    fraud on minority by those in control, 5.32
    generally, 5.26–5.27 5.52
    interests, meaning, 5.45
    just and equitable ground for winding-up, 5.51
    petition, orders under, 5.41–5.44
    *Re Harmer Ltd*, 5.49–5.50
    shareholder agreement, 5.53–5.54
    special majorities, 5.28
    unfairly prejudicial, concept of, 5.46–5.48
  partnership,
    admission of new partner, 5.2–5.3
    court order, dissolution by, 5.23–5.24
    dissolution, 5.22A-5.24
    duties of partner, 5.4
    expulsion of partner, 5.11–5.13
    firm's name, unanimity relating to, 5.9
    generally, 5.25
    good faith, acting in, 5.14–5.15
    injunctions, 5.16–5.18
    majority voting, 5.2–5.3
    management, 5.5–5.6
    manager, appointment of, 5.19–5.21
    partnership agreement, changes in, 5.8
    position of minority partner, 5.1
    ratification of activities falling outside actual authority, 5.10
    receiver, appointment of, 5.19–5.21 5.22
    unanimity, 5.7–5.10
    unanimous decisions, 5.2–5.3
**Misfeasance proceedings**
  grounds upon which brought, 6.94
  liability under, 6.93

**Notice**
  dissolution of partnership by, 3.74–3.75
**Nullity of marriage.** *See* DIVORCE

**Operating enterprise**
  family company,
    articles of association, 2.36
    authority of directors, 2.62
    directors,
      appointment of, 2.34
      authority of, 2.62
      duties of, 2.39
      fiduciary duties, 2.40–2.41
      financial provision, 2.50
      individual shareholders, duties to, 2.43–2.45
      managing director, 2.38
      powers of, 2.35
      removal, 2.53–2.57
      responsibilities, 2.34
      retirement, 2.52
      rules against profiting, 2.42
      termination of office, 2.51
    duties of director, 2.39
    English authority, 2.46–2.47
    fiduciary duties, 2.40–2.41
    financial provision for directors, 2.50
    individual shareholders, duties to, 2.43–2.45
    managing director, 2.38
    nature of, 2.33
    pre-emption rights, 2.58–2.61
    profiting, rules against, 2.42
    reversion of powers to shareholders, 2.37
    shareholder agreements,
      contents, 2.64–2.65
      standard provisions contained in, 2.65
      use of, 2.63 2.66
    shareholders,
      duties between, 2.48
      individual, duties to, 2.43–2.45
      reversion of powers to, 2.37
      voting in best interests of company, 2.49
  partnership,
    accounts, 2.13
    agreement, 2.4–2.9
    arbitration, 2.31
    bankruptcy, 2.22
    death of partner, 2.18–2.19
    decisions, 2.4–2.9
    determination of majority, 2.11
    dissolution, 2.25
    duties of partners, 2.14
    expulsion, 2.23
    illness of partner, 2.29–2.30
    indemnities, 2.17
    insurance, 2.28
    mediation, 2.32
    meetings, provision for, 2.12
    participation in affairs of, 2.2–2.3
    pensions, 2.26–2.27
    pregnancy of partner, 2.29–2.30
    prescribed duties, 2.15–2.16
    retirement of partner, 2.20–2.21
    running business, 2.1
    special majorities, 2.10

**Operating enterprise** – *contd*
partnership – *contd*
termination, consequences of, 2.24
winding up, 2.25
running business, 2.1
special majorities, 2.10

**Partners.** *See* PARTNERSHIP
**Partnership**
accounts,
adjustment of, 3.78–3.81
generally, 2.13
agreement, 2.4–2.9 5.8
arbitration, 2.31
assets, distribution of, 3.78–3.81
bankruptcy of partner, 2.22
consequences of termination, 2.24
court order, dissolution by, 5.23–5.24
death of partner,
beneficiaries, 4.18–4.20
bequest of partnership share, 4.27–4.31
creditors of partnership, 4.12–4.13
debts incurred after, 4.14
generally, 2.18–2.19 4.9–4.11
life interests, 4.32–4.33
loans to partnership, 4.21–4.26
personal representatives admitted as partners, 4.15–4.17
separate creditors, 4.18–4.20
decisions of, 2.4–2.9
determination of majority, 2.11
dissolution,
court order, by, 5.23–5.24
generally, 2.25
minority partner, position of, 5.22A
divorce, effect of,
assignment of partnership share, 3.31–3.35
increase of drawings by partner, 3.21
purchase of partner's share, 3.28–3.29
expulsion of partner, 2.23 5.11–5.13
illness of partner, 2.29–2.30
indemnities, 2.17
insolvent. *See* INSOLVENCY
insurance, 2.28
limited company or,
accounts and reports,
abbreviated, form of, 1.16–1.18
comparative costs, 1.10–1.11
deregulation, new regime for, 1.20
dispensing with laying accounts, 1.18
exemptions and exceptions, 1.12–1.15
medium-sized companies, 1.13–1.15 1.16
small companies, 1.13–1.15 1.17
company auditors, 1.19
comparative costs, 1.9–1.11
discrimination, 1.30
financing business, 1.6
fiscal advantages, 1.7–1.8
generally, 1.1–1.3 1.33
hiving off parts of business, 1.23–1.26
incorporation, 1.21–1.22

**Partnership** – *contd*
limited company or – *contd*
limited liability, 1.4–1.5
mergers, 1.27–1.29
restraint of trade, 1.31–1.32
selling of business in whole or in part, 1.22
social welfare legislation, 1.30
loans to, 4.21–4.26
majority,
determination of, 2.11
special, 2.10
mediation, 2.32
meetings, provision for, 2.12
minority partner,
admission of new partner, 5.2–5.3
court order, dissolution by, 5.23–5.24
dissolution,
court order, by, 5.23–5.24
generally, 5.22A
duties of, 5.4
expulsion of partner, 5.11–5.13
firm's name, 5.9
generally, 5.1 5.25
good faith, 5.14–5.15
injunctions, 5.16–5.18
majority voting, 5.2–5.3
management, 5.5–5.6
manager, appointment of, 5.19–5.21
partnership agreement, changes in provisions in, 5.8
ratification of activities falling outside actual authority, 5.10
receiver, appointment of, 5.19–5.21 5.22
unanimity, 5.7–5.10
unanimous decisions, 5.2–5.3
partners,
bankruptcy, 2.22
death, 2.18–2.19
duties of, 2.14
expulsion, 2.23 5.11–5.13
good faith, acting in, 5.14–5.15
illness of, 2.29–2.30
minority partner. *See* minority partner, *above*
participation in partnership affairs, 2.2–2.3
pensions, 2.26–2.27
pregnancy of, 2.29–2.30
retirement, 2.20–2.21
pensions, 2.26–2.27
post-dissolution profits, 3.77
pregnancy of partner, 2.29–2.30
prescribed duties, 2.15–2.16
retirement of partner, 2.20–2.21
special majorities, 2.10
termination, consequences of, 2.24
winding up,
adjustment of accounts, 3.78–3.81
breach of partnership agreement, 3.73
carried on at loss, 3.73
consequences of, 3.76–3.77
court order, dissolution by, 3.73

**Partnership** – *contd*
winding up – *contd*
destruction of mutual confidence, 3.73
distribution of assets, 3.78–3.81
generally, 2.25 3.70
insolvent partnership, 3.83 6.7–6.8
just and equitable ground, 3.73
notice, dissolution by, 3.74–3.75
Partnership Act 1890, dissolution under, 3.71–3.72
post-dissolution profits, 3.77
rule in *Garner v Murray*, 3.82
**Pensions**
partners, of, 2.26–2.27
**Periodical payments.** *See* DIVORCE
**Petition.** *See* INSOLVENCY
**Post-nuptial settlement**
variation of, 3.44
**Pre-emption rights**
absence of, 2.58
first refusal, right of, 2.59
meaning, 2.58
refusal to register share transfer, 2.60–2.61
**Pregnancy**
partner, of, 2.29–2.30
**Priority of debts.** *See* INSOLVENCY
**Profits**
post-dissolution, 3.77
rules against profiting, 2.42
**Property**
business as, 3.2–3.4
orders for sale of, 3.45
settlement of order, 3.43
transfer of, 3.43
**Provisional liquidator**
appointment of, 3.64

**Qualifying distribution**
advance corporation tax, 1.7

**Receiver**
appointment of, 5.19–5.21 5.22
**Remuneration**
directors, of, effect of divorce on, 3.19
**Reports**
medium-sized companies, 1.16
small companies, 1.17
**Restraint of trade**
enforceability of clauses, 1.32
partnership or company, 1.31–1.32
**Retirement**
director, of, 2.52
partner, of, 2.20–2.21

**Separation.** *See* DIVORCE
**Shareholder agreement**
contents, 2.64–2.65
minority shareholder, protection of, 5.53–5.54
standard provisions contained in, 2.65
use of, 2.63 2.66
**Shareholders**
control,

**Shareholders** – *contd*
control – *contd*
concept of, 5.32
fraud on minority by those in, 5.32
controlling shareholder, death of, 4.4–4.8
death of, 4.2–4.3
duties between, 2.48
individual, duties to, 2.43–2.45
interests, concept of, 5.45
matrimonial disputes, 3.36–3.40
minority,
Companies Act 1985, s 459, 5.37–5.40
directors,
action against, 5.30–5.31
duties of, 5.29
fraud, meaning, 5.33–5.36
fraud on minority by those in control, 5.32
generally, 5.26–5.27 5.52
interests, meaning, 5.45
just and equitable ground for winding-up, 5.51
petition, orders under, 5.41–5.44
*Re Harmer Ltd*, 5.49–5.50
shareholder agreement and, 5.53–5.54
special majorities, 5.28
unfairly prejudicial, concept of, 5.46–5.48
reversion of powers to, 2.37
voting in best interests of company, 2.49
**Shares**
pre-emption rights, 2.58–2.61
purchase by company of its own shares, 3.22–3.24
shareholders. *See* SHAREHOLDERS
third party, sale to, 3.30
**Small companies**
abbreviated accounts and reports, form of, 1.17
accounting requirements, exemptions and exceptions to, 1.13–1.15
**Social welfare**
partnership or company, 1.30
**Spouses**
divorce. *See* DIVORCE
matrimonial disputes, 3.36–3.40

**Taxation**
maintenance payments, 3.11–3.13
partnership or company, 1.7–1.8
purchase by company of its own shares, 3.25–3.27
**Third party**
sale of shares to, 3.30
**Trading**
fraudulent, 6.88–6.89
wrongful, 6.90–6.92

**Voluntary liquidation.** *See* WINDING UP
**Voting**
partnership,
determination of majority, 2.11
special majorities, 2.10

**Voting** – *contd*
  shareholders, by, 2.49
  special majorities, 5.28

**Winding up**
  circumstances of, 3.62–3.63
  commencement of, 3.65–3.66
  compulsory liquidation, 3.61
  creditors' voluntary liquidation,
    generally, 3.58
    liquidation committee, 3.59–3.60
  death of member, on, 4.36
  dissolution of company,
    generally, 3.67
    voluntary liquidation, completion of, 3.68–3.69
  insolvent partnership, 3.83 6.7–6.8
  just and equitable ground for, 5.51
  liquidator,
    appointment of, 3.54–3.57
    provisional, appointment of, 3.64
  meaning, 3.48
  members' voluntary liquidation,
    generally, 3.49
    liquidator, appointment of, 3.54–3.57
    nature of declaration, 3.50–3.52

**Winding up** – *contd*
  members' voluntary liquidation – *contd*
    resolution for, 3.53
  notice, dissolution by, 3.74–3.75
  partnership,
    adjustment of accounts, 3.78–3.81
    breach of partnership agreement, 3.73
    carried on at loss, 3.73
    consequences of, 3.76–3.77
    court order, dissolution by, 3.73
    destruction of mutual confidence, 3.73
    distribution of assets, 3.78–3.81
    generally, 2.25 3.70
    insolvent, 3.83 6.7–6.8
    just and equitable ground, 3.73
    notice, dissolution by, 3.74–3.75
    Partnership Act 1890, dissolution under, 3.71–3.72
    post-dissolution profits, 3.77
    rule in *Garner v Murray*, 3.82
  provisional liquidator, appointment of, 3.64
  solvent liquidation, 3.48
  *See also* INSOLVENCY

**Wrongful trading**
  proceedings relating to, 6.90–6.92